A MANAGER'S GUIDE

CLIENT

SERVER

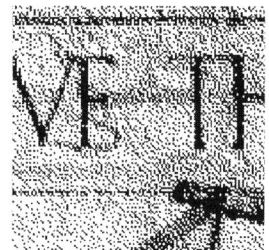

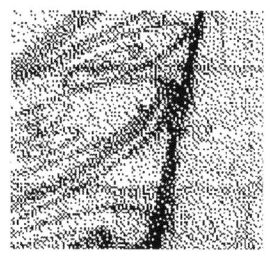

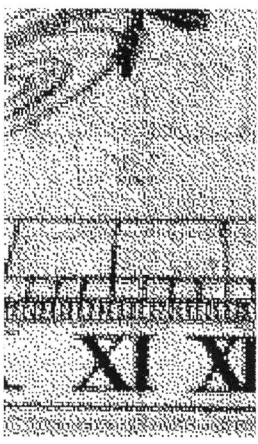

A MANAGER'S GUIDE

CLIENT

SERVER

LAURENCE SHAFE Ph.D.

proven client/server solutions

Boston London Frankfurt

Addison-Wesley Publishing Company

Wokingham, England • Reading, Massachusetts • Menlo Park, California
New York • Don Mills, Ontario • Amsterdam • Bonn • Sydney • Singapore
Tokyo • Madrid • San Juan • Milan • Paris • Mexico City • Seoul • Taipei

The information and material contained in this book are provided 'as is', without warranty of any
kind, expressed or implied, including without limitation any warranty concerning the accuracy,
adequacy, or completeness of such information or material or the results to be obtained from
using such information or material. Neither Intelligent Environments nor the author shall be
responsible for any claims attributable to errors, omissions, or other inaccuracies in the
information or material contained in this book, and in no event shall Intelligent Environments or
the author be liable for direct, indirect, special, incidental, or consequential damages arising out of
the use of such information or material. Any opinions expressed are those of Intelligent
Environments and are based on information in the public domain at the time of writing.

Many of the designations used by manufacturers and sellers to distinguish their products are
claimed as trademarks. Addison-Wesley has made every attempt to supply trademark information
about manufacturers and their products mentioned in this book. A list of the trademark
designations and their owners appears on page xiv.

Cover and half-title page designed by op den Brouw Design and Illustration,
Reading, incorporating photograph © Telegraph Colour Library by
Roger Antrobus and printed by The Riverside Printing Co. (Reading) Ltd.
Typeset by Tradespools Ltd., Frome, Somerset.
Printed and bound in Great Britain at Biddles of Guildford.

First printed 1994

ISBN 0-201-42790-7

British Library Cataloguing-in-Publication Data
A catalogue record for this book is available from the British Library.

Library of Congress Cataloguing-in-Publication Data is available

To my mother and father;
and Valerie, Anna and Oliver.
For all your love.

Foreword

I am delighted to write the foreword to this book as I have followed the work of Laurence Shafe and his team at Intelligent Environments since the initial development of IBM OS/2 Version 1.0. The successful employment of Intelligent Environments' AM development tool by corporations worldwide has contributed to the success of OS/2. The strengths of OS/2 combined with the development productivity gains achievable using AM have powerful and innovative new applications for the personal computer.

Laurence Shafe has produced in this book, an informative and, at times, very entertaining overview of OS/2, contemporary programming methodologies, and AM. I recommend that this book be read by anyone planning to develop PC-based applications for running their business.

Following the introduction of IBM OS/2 Version 2.1 during 1993, tremendous new opportunities avail themselves to users of 32-bit IBM-compatible personal computers. Users now have the freedom of choice of selecting and running concurrently under OS/2 2.1, the applications that best suit their need from the wide array of 16-bit DOS, Windows and OS/2 commercially available applications. In addition, well over 1,000 32-bit OS/2 applications are already under development by software companies worldwide. But very importantly, tools such as AM allow companies to produce custom applications which can provide them with a competitive business advantage. Just read this book to see how many of the world's prominent companies have done just that!

OS/2 Version 2.1 is designed and priced for use by people running DOS-based applications, yet who need many of the constraints of DOS removed. And, at no additional charge, OS/2 2.1 runs Windows-based and OS/2-based applications concurrently within Windows on the same screen as the DOS applications. This is great! But this new, 32-bit operating system, with object-oriented technology for the end user and the programmer built-in, opens up a new world of innovative easy-to-use functions. And Intelligent Environments' AM is here to help you explore this new world.

I hope you enjoy reading this book as much as I did and I wish you every success from the use of OS/2.

John A. Soyring
Director, Software Development Programs
International Business Machines, Corp.

Preface

Client/Server: A Manager's Guide is the successor to *OS/2 in the Corporate Environment*, which was read by over 100 000 people around the world. The widespread success of the first book bears witness to the need for more easily understood, independent, information about what is happening in the fast-changing world of client/server. What started as a minor update has turned into a major rewrite that has resulted in this book.

Most of the sections have been rewritten and the book has been restructured to make it easier to follow. I have included details of Microsoft 32-bit Windows strategy and updated the OS/2 section to cover OS/2 2.1 with a discussion of the role of Workplace OS. I have also omitted the section on IBM's AD/Cycle and rewritten the chapters on development tools and project methodology.

The purpose of this book is to try to unravel the implications of client/server computing for those organizations wondering whether and how to get started. It is focused on corporate client/server applications that run the business, rather than on departmental support systems. It is aimed at business managers and professionals involved with software applications, as well as IT professionals and users who want to keep abreast of the latest trends and issues.

The goals of the book are to help you, the reader:

- Decide on operating systems for the desktop (Windows, OS/2 or UNIX).

- Unravel the complexities of accessing mainframe data.

- See what sort of systems are possible.

- Understand the risks and advantages of Object-Oriented Programming.

- Select the best development tools for your business.

- Plan, design and manage your client/server projects.

- Understand what client/server is really all about.

I have tried to state clearly my personal opinion on all the major issues rather than just present a summary of the facts. I have done this because I believe all organizations, large and small, must be making major Information Technology (IT) decisions now to stay in business and be competitive. Making decisions is difficult and I believe it is helpful to hear an opinion rather than just a set of dry facts.

The key battles taking place in the market today will determine the standard operating systems of the future, as well as the hardware architecture and the role of the developer. Working in a development tools company has given me a broad perspective of the market. I have seen many graphical client/server applications developed in the financial, industrial, and government sectors. This has given me a view on how this type of development can incorporate the needs of the developer, the management services department and the end-user.

I believe that in ten years' time we will look back on the early 1990s as an exciting period. It was the time we started using PCs to integrate all users' systems, the time when important decisions were made and big changes took place.

The major technical decisions that must be made today are the choice of operating system, the way in which data is accessed and the selection of development tools. As you will find, I believe that the operating system for corporate client/server applications needs to be 32-bit, multitasking and stable, with good SQL database and communications support.

The more difficult and important decision, however, concerns software development tools. Effective software development tools result in systems that achieve business objectives, make the user more effective, isolate the application from the underlying software and hardware and that can be modified and reused as business changes.

However, if there is a single message to take out of all this technical analysis, it is to forget it, and focus on the end-user. Choose an operating environment that provides the most intuitive and effective support for their job, use methodologies that are end-user oriented and get on with it.

Dr Laurence Shafe
Chief Executive
Intelligent Environments

Contents

CHAPTER 1

WHY CLIENT/SERVER?

Fashions come and go in the computer industry, yet real changes take place behind the marketing hype. This book explores some current concepts and tries to untangle the fact from the fashion.

The technical terms 'client' and 'server' have been used for many years but since the late 1980s the term 'client/server' has come to have special significance – it represents a trend. Simply speaking, this trend is towards all applications being run on a PC with a graphical user interface (GUI) and accessing data across a network. If this is all there were to client/server computing then this book would simply be about local area networks (LANs) and the cost-effectiveness of resource sharing.

However, it also concerns a bigger revolution that is taking place – the implementation of what I call 'high-end' client/server applications. High-end client/server applications read and write corporate data, typically from a mainframe (see Figure 1.1), but often from a mid-range UNIX machine or AS/400.

As 80% of the mainframes in the world are IBM compatible, this book has a strong IBM orientation when describing the communications and database requirements.

The other important distinction between client/server and high-end client/server is that high-end applications are critical to your business, that is, if the application stops, your business also stops. These are sometimes called 'mission-critical' applications and they demand the highest standards of reliability and performance from the operating system and from development tools.

So the question 'why client/server?' should be 'why high-end client/server?',

1

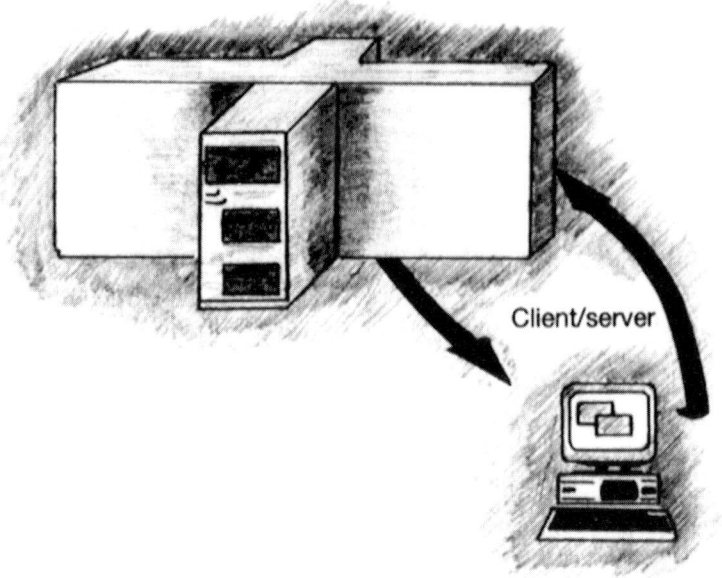

Figure 1.1 High-end client/server application.

that is, why implement applications on a PC when previously they were implemented on a mainframe? There are many answers to this, but essentially it is to make the user more effective by providing a more responsive interface to corporate information.

This may sound like a modest objective but it is actually profound. It is an entirely different objective from that of most current mainframe applications. Their justification is based on processing business transactions more cost-effectively. In order to ensure the application maximizes the effectiveness of the user, a new approach is needed to the application development process. This is why the trend towards client/server goes hand-in-hand with the trend towards prototyping and joint application development (JAD) with the users.

The development of high-end client/server applications is a complex task. The programming effort required in any third-generation language (3GL), such as COBOL, C or C++, is one to two orders of magnitude more than would be required for a mainframe application. For example, there are several thousand different functions provided by the operating system just to manipulate the GUI. In addition, the architecture and data access are more complex than for an application running on a mainframe. This is why the trend towards high-end client/server is accompanied by a trend towards the use of fourth-generation languages (4GLs).

The use of a 4GL brings many other benefits. Not only does it reduce development costs but it also makes JAD possible, reduces training costs when switching staff from mainframe development to client/server development and results in applications that are easier to maintain. Maintenance of existing mainframe applications is a major burden on most information technology (IT) departments and the use of a 3GL to develop client/server applications would result in this burden becoming intolerable over the next few years.

In the past, applications automated the processing of existing manual systems. Client/server applications often change the way the business operates and this goes to the heart of their business justification. The answer to 'why high-end client/server?' is 'to keep your business competitive by enabling your employees to provide new levels of service both internally and externally'.

A PC with a GUI provides an easy-to-use interface, a consistent interface across applications, and a fast and flexible way of presenting a wealth of complex, changing information at a glance. The justification of the cost of providing such an interface comes from the business benefits this can bring. It is the responsibility of each IT manager to think how such a technology can be used to change and enhance the business.

This change to a PC with a GUI is associated with a change in the role of the user of the application. A dumb terminal is perfect for rapid head-down data entry but unsuitable as a way of presenting and controlling fast-changing data. 'Why client/server?' is another way of asking 'why give staff more information in an easily assimilated and controllable way?'. This makes it a business question and one you should be able to answer for your own organization. How can your business benefit from providing your staff with more information in an easily controlled and flexible way? The answer is to look at those areas of your business that give you a business edge and think where more information, better presented, could improve that edge.

As an example, consider your order-taking operation. If you have a salesforce entering orders on to forms that are then keyed into your mainframe order entry system, would it be better to have a telemarketing force that takes orders directly over the phone?

This illustrates another aspect of client/server – it often changes the way your business operates. In the past, computer systems automated the existing business. Technology, and in particular client/server, increasingly helps to redefine the business.

IT is vital to get and stay in front. More and more we shall see IT driven not by the MIS or DP department but by users, sales people and business managers. They work to timescales of 12 to 24 months and need solutions quickly. It is difficult for anyone to predict business more than 18 months ahead. This means that the lifetime of a business application is under two years. We have to think very differently about managing and implementing these business applications.

Technology is becoming cheaper and cheaper but the choices are multiplying. How can a stable IT base be found with memory prices dropping and processor power rising? Will these factors leave us, in a few years time, with dead-end solutions? Look at the trend:

- The 1960s saw the introduction of commercial batch computer processing.

- The 1970s saw the move to on-line processing using dumb terminals and the growth in the use of the minicomputer.

- The 1980s saw the arrival of the desktop/personal computer – host applications were unchanged. During the 1980s the PC revolution enabled individuals to perform their jobs better and to improve the quality of what they did. PCs became responsive tools adding value to individual tasks throughout an organization – they helped to make money rather than save it. But PCs on their own were limited.

- The 1990s will see the integration of host and personal computer applications and the processing will be carried out where it makes most sense.

Studies have shown that when used as a personal productivity tool, a PC generates a return on investment (ROI) of between 5 and 15%. A higher ROI comes from using PCs in applications that provide direct competitive advantage in the business. Where workstations have been used in isolated areas, up to 300% ROI has been achieved. (The term 'workstation' is used here to mean any desktop computer with a graphical user interface and a processor at least as powerful as an Intel 386.) In companies such as American Airlines, Wells Fargo and Frito-Lay, where the whole business is built around competitive advantage, the flexibility and accuracy of the pervasive use of PCs can provide ROI up to 1000%.

Some companies are satisfied if they reduce IT costs each year, but even if they halve the costs (difficult without increasing service and support costs), then they only improve the ROI from, say, 10% to 20% – and this is not enough for the 1990s. By providing applications that directly support the business rather than productivity tools such as word processors and spreadsheets, it is possible to increase the ROI to 300%.

The big growth area is connecting PCs into local area networks (LANs). These LANs are becoming the foundation for major business applications based on client/server technology. At the same time, proprietary databases are being replaced by standard SQL databases. One LAN can, in the right circumstances, replace a mid-range or mainframe installation.

This is not a strategy for 'throwing out the mainframe'. Sometimes that is the right thing to do, but it must be remembered that the basic systems of a large organization, representing millions of lines of COBOL code, cannot be replaced overnight. The mainframe can still be the best solution for holding and protecting the corporate database and running the basic corporate systems.

Yet despite the case for mainframes, the move to the use of PCs is overwhelming. Today approximately two-thirds of data-processing expenditure is on PCs and it is estimated that this will grow to three-quarters in two to three years.

Despite the amount spent on PCs, they are being under-utilized. The PC could be used to deliver a new generation of corporate applications that have a flexibility and responsiveness that is impossible to deliver with dumb terminals attached to a mainframe. When the interactive, responsive quality of the PC is combined with the massive strength of the corporate database, then the whole organization is made more effective. This is the aim of client/server computing.

In today's software environment, 70% to 80% of development costs are spent on maintaining existing software. This equates to $30 billion spent each year just on maintaining software, and there is currently an average backlog of four years for new software development.

Client/server development is complex and requires new skills. The GUI involves hundreds of function calls to perform what used to take a single function call on the mainframe. It is therefore much more important to use high-level tools for client/server development compared with mainframe development. These tools must support the object-oriented user interface, access corporate data on a mainframe, support interactive development with users and deliver industrial strength applications. Above all, such tools must be easy to learn and use, and must enable software to be reused after it has been developed.

This book expands and comments on this critical technology. The aim is to maximize business effectiveness, and those that use the technology correctly will be the winners in the business battles of the 1990s.

Summary

It is necessary to distinguish between client/server – connecting PCs on a network – and high-end client/server. High-end client/server means rethinking the way in which information is distributed, accessed and presented, and also the way in which applications are developed and the tools used to develop them.

The justification for high-end client/server is based on making the business more profitable by making the user more effective. The application of the technology is up to each organization to determine.

The remainder of this book is about the issues, methods and techniques required to implement effective high-end client/server applications. From now on the term client/server will be used to mean high-end client/server.

CHAPTER 2

CLIENT/SERVER ARCHITECTURES

In many companies the backlog of development work for mainframe applications is measured in years. However, as the business needs ever more new systems to respond to competitive pressure, so the DP department comes under increasing pressure to deliver solutions quickly. At the same time budgets are being squeezed, making it difficult even to keep up with the continual burden of maintenance.

'Down-sizing' is presented as the solution: replace mainframes with minis or PC LANs, thus saving money, and make development more responsive by using the latest type of development tools.

Down-sizing the mainframe

There are two uses of the term 'down-sizing': one refers to replacing mainframes by mid-range machines, typically running UNIX; the other to the process of converting applications to run on networks of smaller computers, typically PCs.

The first trend is often motivated by the wrong objectives. To understand this, consider an organization with a central management information system (MIS) department and many user departments which it services. From the point of view of the user departments, each year the MIS department costs a large amount of money and the benefits are often hard to perceive, especially if it has a long development backlog and is felt to be providing poor service.

Thus it appears to individual user departments that a great deal of money could be saved by managing their information systems themselves. They reason that the cost of a mid-range computer is far lower than the amount they pay to MIS each year, and even with the cost of a few extra staff they think it looks like a good way of saving money. However, if an organization allows each user department to operate in isolation, the result will often be the creation of what are effectively many small MIS departments and the overall cost to the organization will be greater. The inevitable solution will then be to set up one central MIS department and close down all the small units. *Plus ça change, plus c'est la même chose.*

The second meaning of down-sizing is synonymous with the way I've used the term client/server in this book. The benefits of this form of down-sizing come not from cost saving but from making the organization more effective – that is to say, it is to do with *making money*, not saving money.

When a large business is based around a mainframe and suites of applications have been developed over the last 10 to 20 years, then it will not be easy or even desirable to change. Instead you should be planning a layer of LAN-based applications, which will enable you to provide better service through the rapid delivery of more responsive applications, and allow the mainframe applications to continue to run the underlying business.

If the corporate data is to remain on the mainframe, then one of the key technical problems becomes how to organize applications to access and update it.

Accessing corporate data

The key requirements for accessing corporate data from a PC are listed in Table 2.1. These are the same requirements that have been applied for years to on-line transaction processing (OLTP) systems.

The best architecture that satisfies these requirements depends largely on the source of the data. There are three data sources that will be considered, as shown in Table 2.2. Each of these data sources will be considered in turn and a number of methods for accessing such a data source from a PC will be considered with respect to the basic requirements.

1. Existing application screens

How many users log into one mainframe, scribble down some data, then log into another, do the same and finally key the information into a PC spreadsheet

Table 2.1 Requirements for corporate data access.

1. Links to existing data source

2. Easy to program and use

3. High performance and high availability

4. Preserves data reliability and integrity

5. Secure

6. Simple to administer

to calculate the result? If your data comes from existing application screens then a graphical workstation enables it to be picked off the screens automatically and behind the scenes.

'Screen renovation' or 'screen-scraping' refers to this technique of front-ending an existing 3270- or 5250-based application with a graphical user interface (see Figure 2.1). This has proved to be an effective way for many organizations to add value to their existing applications. A project of this type can be started with just one or two staff members, there is no impact on the mainframe systems and it doesn't matter where or how the data is stored. The mainframe application takes care of all that.

Screen renovation can be implemented using the terminal emulation services (called EHLLAPI) of OS/2 Communications Manager or any of a wide variety of Windows products. These turn the workstation into a 3270, as far as the mainframe is concerned.

The workstation running the application can either connect directly to the mainframe (through a modem or direct local link) or a group of workstations on a LAN can all connect through a single modem on a communications server/gateway, such as SNA Server for Windows.

The multi-tasking and multi-programming facilities of the operating system enable an application to control the emulator, extract information from the simulated 3270 screen, add information to the screen and simulate the keyboard. This highlights both the main strength and the main weakness of this approach.

Table 2.2 Accessing data.

1. Existing application screens

2. Distributed access to SQL data

3. Transaction processing

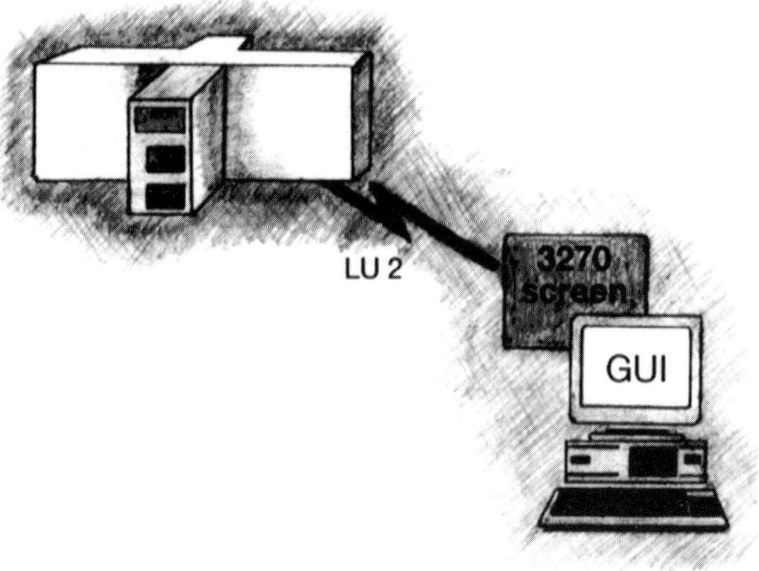

Figure 2.1 Screen renovation.

The approach is non-intrusive, as far as the mainframe is concerned – just another 3270 terminal has been added. The problem is that a 3270 is designed to be used by a person, not controlled by a program. The program must therefore handle messages from the mainframe operator, system down status, menus and form filling designed for people, and pauses and delays caused by varying response times from the mainframe. The slightest hiccup (for example, a line error or a change to the host application) can result in the PC sending incorrect character sequences to the host application. Imagine your order entry system hit by a blast of invalid characters. Anything could happen – invalid values entered, orders deleted, addresses overwritten and so on. However if the application is only reading data, then these dangers do not arise, so screen renovation is useful for decision support applications.

The PC application must be kept in line with changes made to the mainframe application, and both the PC and the mainframe application should do extensive validity checking to make sure they do not become out of step.

This approach is the best way to upgrade or enhance existing host systems but is, at best, a shaky foundation on which to base a line-of-business application. Many organizations start this way before moving on to full client/server application development.

Advantages

(1) Screen renovation is simple and easy to implement, with little interference to the operation of the mainframe system.

(2) It enables information from many mainframes to be easily combined on to a single screen. This is valuable for those users who must log on to different mainframe systems and manually write down data.

(3) It is possible to combine this method with others as a means of obtaining particular data, such as that from a VSAM file used by an existing mainframe application.

Disadvantages

(1) If screen renovation is used to send data, then the validation at the mainframe end should be very tight. If the program gets out of step with the screens, it can 'randomly' send keystrokes to the application. This danger can also be minimized by the application checking the current screen status before every update.

(2) The program must cope with the rigors of handling an interface designed for a person using a terminal and keyboard. Strict maintenance control must be placed on any change to the mainframe 3270 screens as corresponding changes must be made to the client programs. Performance problems can be expected with large numbers of attached workstations running multiple 3270 sessions.

(3) Screen renovation is not a 'strategic' solution in the sense that there is no future progression to new systems, no migration route to other architectures and no system control of security and data integrity.

2. Distributed access to SQL data

All the major SQL database vendors have a strategy for transparent, distributed data access and control. However, all are a long way from achieving this goal. As an example, IBM's strategy will be described as it encompasses the most important SQL mainframe database – but all of the vendors, such as Oracle and Sybase, have similar strategies.

IBM's strategy is based on an open, transparent, distributed access architecture called DRDA (Distributed Relational Database Architecture). DRDA is a published standard which a number of third-party database vendors have committed to support. DRDA will be implemented in three stages:

- Remote unit of work (RUW)
- Distributed unit of work (DUW)
- Distributed request

The RUW means that only one database can be accessed at a time, but that database can be remote. The DUW enables multiple distributed databases to be accessed, but each SQL statement may only refer to a single database (this requires what is sometimes called 'two-phase commit' to preserve database integrity). The final stage implies multiple distributed databases, including joining tables from different databases.

The first stage (RUW) has already been achieved and is implemented by a product called DDCS/2. DDCS/2 provides transparent read and write access to the IBM relational databases for both static and dynamic SQL (see below) with full cursor support.

Mainframe applications run on the same machine as the database and the use of remote 3270 terminals results in relatively few characters being sent across the network. The architecture for remote SQL access means splitting the system between the database and the application. The communication between these parts consists of SQL requests sent in one direction and data returned in the other. The application generally runs on the same machine as the user interface and so it can be extremely responsive.

DDCS/2 runs on the client machines and re-directs SQL requests to a local or remote relational database. The re-direction is controlled by a directory of database locations and so can be changed dynamically without changing the application. The databases currently supported are DB2/2, DB2 under MVS, SQL/DS under VM, the OS/400 SQL database and DB2/6000. To the application it appears that the database is local.

DDCS/2 supports multiple remote units of work to a single database. It does not support a single unit of work accessing tables across multiple databases. The use of DDCS/2 is most suitable for new applications being developed that need to read and update a central SQL database directly. DDCS/2 should revolution-ize the way DB2 is accessed as it enables PC applications to access it as easily as mainframe applications.

It is important that if you are updating your corporate IBM database from a workstation you should involve your mainframe database administrator and plan to use static SQL for security and performance reasons.

IBM relational databases handle two types of SQL access – static and dynamic (Figure 2.2). Dynamic access requires the complete SQL statement to be sent from the application to the database machine, where it is interpreted. The interpretation involves compiling the statement and determining the best physical access plan to access the data. Dynamic SQL is only suitable for *ad hoc* inquiries, typically of the type generated by an executive information system. For security and performance reasons it should not be used to update data (even though this is possible).

Static SQL is for production applications. It offers first-class security, data integrity and high performance. Static SQL is pre-compiled and stored in the database as an 'access plan'. It is efficient and much more secure than dynamic SQL, and is also suitable if the SQL statements are pre-defined, as they are in a transaction-based application. The security stems from the fact that it is possible to be set up so that only the pre-defined static SQL statements can be executed by a user. If users are allowed to enter dynamic SQL, then there is much less control over what they are able to do. For example, with dynamic SQL, a user who sends a request taking 0.2 second to select data from a 100 000 row table cannot be prevented from doing a 'correlated sub-query' that could take 6 hours! It is therefore essential to use static SQL when building transaction-based systems.

The improved performance comes about because the SQL access has been pre-defined by the DBA and the best physical access plan has already been determined by the compiler/optimizer. Performance is also improved by the

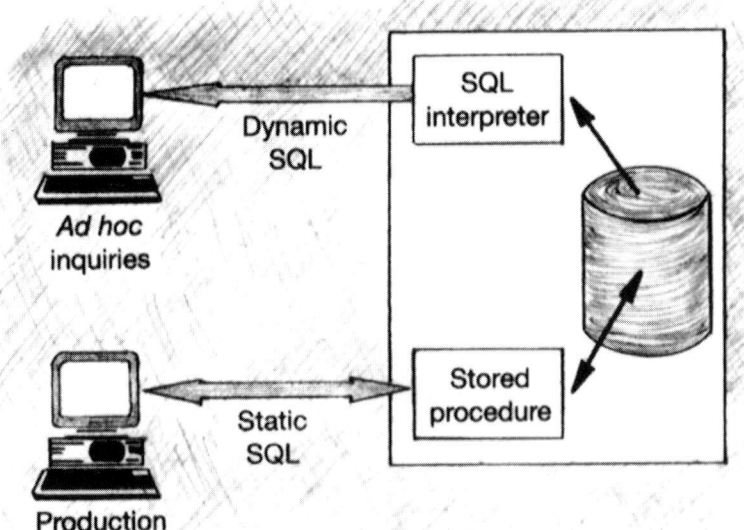

Figure 2.2 IBM SQL access.

reduction in the size of the SQL request across the communications network. This can be considerable as a single dynamic statement can be several kilobytes and the equivalent static request a few bytes. A highly tuned static SQL request can be 10 times faster than the worst equivalent dynamic SQL request, for the same physical database structure.

Static SQL requests are fully secure as security is associated with the user, the program and the particular table columns. An example will show how important this is. If a program uses dynamic SQL to update a salary column, then the *user* must be given permission to update the salary column. However, that same user could then use any general query tool (such as a spreadsheet) to change any salary, and do so without any cross-check or audit trail!

If the program uses static SQL, the user could be restricted to run only that program (strictly speaking, the user is restricted to using a particular set of database access plans). The program can cross-check and validate all changes, and maintain an audit trail. The user will not be given permission to update the database directly and so any attempt to update a table using a general query tool will be rejected.

Other SQL databases can be accessed remotely in a similar way and a number of third-party database gateways are available. The principle behind these gateway products involves 'intercepting' raw SQL requests issued by a workstation application and routing them through gateway software on the LAN to the particular SQL database.

A number of such products exist today, for example MicroDecisionWare's DB Gateway and SequeLink from TechGnosis. Sybase and Oracle also have their own support for accessing their databases across a local or wide area network.

It should not be forgotten that an alternative which is sometimes most cost-effective is to down-load the data overnight into your local SQL database. You can then use local SQL to access that data during the day. This approach is ideal for static data or tables that rarely change.

Advantages

(1) The use of a gateway is transparent to the application. No communications programming is required, just SQL. In particular, DRDA is an architecture that will continue to be well supported by IBM in the future.

(2) The advantage of using the IBM databases is that they are all compatible and scalable. Because they are compatible, a client application can be written and tested against a local DB2/2 copy of the DB2 database and then, at a later stage, switched to the production DB2 database. This switch does not involve any code changes.

(3) Compatability also allows an application server to grow from DB2/2 running on a PC, to DB2/6000 on a mid-range machine, to DB2 on a mainframe.

Disadvantages

(1) The organization does require experience of SQL as there are many performance pitfalls that arise from its seductive ease of use. However, if the requirement is to link to DB2 then this experience will already exist. It is important such experience is brought to bear on the design and use of SQL from the workstation, even with local DB2/2 databases.

(2) The use of SQL to access remote data through a gateway can suffer from performance problems compared with a transaction-based approach, especially if dynamic SQL is used. Every SQL statement involves a separate trip to the mainframe and back.

(3) If the mainframe database is DB2 then every program has an open link to DB2 called a thread. Each thread requires resources on the mainframe. Typically, in a CICS environment there might be 30 threads open at any one time as CICS transactions flow through the mainframe. For 500 workstations, each with, say, two programs accessing DB2, there will be 1000 threads – a considerable (30-fold) increase! Some development tools recognize this potential problem and will automatically 'time-out' the SQL connection.

(4) Another important design consideration is defining the logical unit of work (LUW, a self-consistent set of SQL requests). An LUW should not remain open too long, certainly not while the user goes to lunch! This can arise if the applications are not well designed and standards are not enforced during programming.

(5) Many of these performance considerations do not arise when a transaction processing monitor, such as CICS, is used.

3. Transaction processing

For nearly 30 years, organizations have relied on IBM's CICS to provide secure, dependable, high-performance access to distributed corporate data. The requirements listed in Table 2.1 are the basic requirements for all transaction-processing systems, such as CICS.

There are many different terms used to describe the architecture used by CICS – transaction-based, peer-to-peer and cooperative processing, for example. The essence of the approach is that processing is divided into units, called transactions, and these can be processed on any machine in the network. This gives great configuration flexibility and scalability, and it splits the processing load more evenly between the systems. It also hides the data access inside one of the applications. The architecture has a lot in common with a distributed object-based approach.

A transaction could be processed on a PC, a mid-range machine or a mainframe. Each machine in the network should be doing what it is best suited to. Obviously a PC is good at intensive, responsive user interaction and a mainframe at database processing, as it can handle vast amounts of data. The application logic could be processed on a mid-range server, an architecture called the 'three layer' approach.

A transaction-based approach means that the application must be analysed and 'split' at a higher level than the database access commands. This level is often described as the transaction level and it corresponds to a single business operation. In relational database terms this would typically be a logical unit of work.

The architecture requires a communications environment that can handle large volumes of transactions between applications on different types of machine.

Also considered in this section is APPC, a communications protocol that is supported on a wide range of IBM and non-IBM machines. It is a low-level method to use compared with CICS but has the advantage of being supported on a wider range of machines.

CICS

IBM's CICS (Customer Information Control System) is available for a range of IBM and UNIX machines. It provides the capability for one program to call another anywhere on the network. One program calls the other as if it were local, and all the network routing is handled by CICS.

With conventional OLTP, transactions are sent from the periphery (usually from non-programmable terminals) to a central system which is optimized for maximum transaction throughput.

Client/server replaces the OLTP architecture with one in which any processor can send a transaction to any other, and request that it perform some action (see Figure 2.3). The benefits of this approach are:

- A fast, responsive user interface, controlled locally with a fast and consistent response time for the processing of remote transactions.

- The application logic is dealt with independently of database access, allowing a mixture of SQL and non-SQL databases to be combined. (It is estimated that over half of the corporate data that exists is stored in VSAM files.)

- Application logic can be run on the host computer, including control and batch programs.

- Loading on the communications line is low, as only transaction messages are sent and the minimum amount of data returned. A high volume of transactions can be processed by the network.

- The 'ACID' properties are supported. These are the fundamental properties of data integrity, namely, Atomicity (transactions are guaranteed to run to completion or to have no effect at all), Consistency (any data updates made change the data from one consistent state to another), Isolation (transactions can be written as if they were processed serially even though they are run concurrently) and Durability (once a transaction is finished its changes are never lost even if there is a total system failure).

- The corporate data is protected physically and operationally by a department dedicated to the task. Such mainframe OLTP systems often run non-stop 24 hours a day, seven days a week.

If the workstation applications communicate directly with the mainframe, then the best solution is to use IBM's CICS for Windows or CICS for OS/2 product and write the mainframe applications under CICS in, for example, COBOL. The CICS program running on the mainframe will pick up the data from the transaction and carry out the necessary SQL or VSAM file retrieval operations to perform the unit of work and return the data to the workstation.

The programming interface is supplied as part of CICS and it enables a program

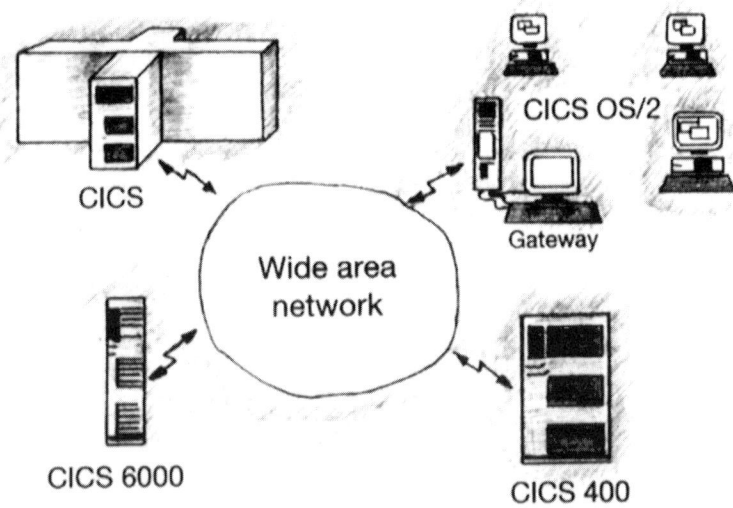

Figure 2.3 A typical CICS network.

to call any CICS transaction (local or remote) and send or receive a buffer or table of information in the transaction's communication area. Using this as an application can execute a host–resident CICS transaction against DB2 (or anything else – VSAM, IMS and so on).

CICS requires no explicit communication coding (although CICS uses APPC/LU6.2 for its underlying communications). Often an organization will have already written many of the required CICS transactions and the graphical front-end applications can be introduced into the same architecture. However, to do this smoothly requires the CICS programs to be written as small transactions that are independent of the CICS user interface. The biggest advantage of this approach is that it is a simple solution for CICS customers, since workstation applications can call existing transactions, and it is easy to create new ones.

The statistics of CICS are remarkable – over 490 of IBM's top 500 customers use CICS, there are over 2000 CICS packages offered by over 1000 vendors worldwide and over 36 000 CICS licenses are in use by an estimated 300 000 CICS programmers in over 90 countries. CICS runs on all the major IBM mainframe operating systems, as well as 32-bit Windows, OS/2, IBM's AS/400 range, and the RS/6000 and other UNIX machines.

CICS has been going through some revolutionary and remarkable changes recently and it looks as though it could become IBM's single standard for transaction processing in the future. In a recent survey, IDC forecast that these changes would mean that the CICS share of the TP monitor market would grow from 54% in 1992 to 65% in 1997.

APPC

System Network Architecture (SNA) is IBM's strategic standard for communications. An important SNA concept is that of logical units, or LUs. An LU can be compared to a socket into which a user or an application can plug itself. A network provides services that connect logical units together. There are currently seven types of SNA logical unit numbered from 0 through 7 (type 5 is spare). As the functions that a logical unit can perform are enhanced, version numbers are added. So LU 6.2 is the latest definition of the capabilities of a type 6 logical unit. LU 6.2 is used to implement a set of functions called advanced program-to-program communication (or APPC for short).

APPC is IBM's strategic peer-to-peer communication protocol. It enables two programs on separate machines to have a 'conversational' send-and-receive session. The programs on each machine will have to 'understand' and manage the APPC communications, and each transaction can do whatever it has been programmed to do. APPC gives:

- Good control of the conversations and their reliability.

- An efficient solution that is independent of server location.

- Support for a wide range of IBM and non-IBM machines.

APPC is a very robust but inflexible communications protocol which unfortunately has become a widely used standard for all types of communication. It is excellent for connecting systems involving a small number of connections but many transactions, such as connecting a LAN to a mainframe through a gateway. It is less suitable as a simple workstation-to-workstation protocol, although this has been partly addressed by the latest LAN-only version which provides high performance across a LAN with low overheads.

Some organizations have little experience with APPC and imagine that it is highly complex. In fact, the entire verb set is no greater than 40 or so, and excellent programming interfaces are available.

Some development tools handle the entire workstation communications activity automatically (with default parameters and processing). Such tools support state management, data type conversion, buffer processing and handle multiple sessions.

At the host, you can create APPC-handling transaction partners in a variety of ways (for example, MVS CICS COBOL or AS/400). Correctly designed, with LAN traffic directed through a gateway to the host, APPC can be a fast, compact communications protocol for implementing your own transaction-based architecture.

Advantages

(1) The advantages of a transaction-based architecture are flexibility and performance. The flexibility comes from the way in which the communication is packaged into business units. The location or method of processing those units may change but the transactions themselves do not need to.

(2) In the longer term, IBM's new open cross-platform CICS strategy could make this a significant option for client/server implementation.

(3) Those seeking an approach that takes them from transaction-based on APPC today to a CICS approach in the future should consider building the application around a higher level architecture, such as that supported by some development tools.

Disadvantages

(1) Transaction-based approaches are technically more complex and difficult to implement. They also require the organization to analyse its application requirements in transaction terms. Both these activities require time and expertise at the beginning of the project and so may delay timescales and increase costs.

(2) An organization needs the right level of technical expertise, both to design and to implement the underlying architecture.

Summary

Screen renovation allows a new application to be developed quickly and easily with the minimum disruption to the mainframe environment. However, it is not a sound architecture around which to base a long-term client/server architecture. It is the method an organization would use if it wanted a quick way of getting an initial proof-of-concept application working.

Direct SQL access is transparent and simple and does not involve any mainframe programming. However, care must be taken when designing the architecture to minimize the load placed on the mainframe and the consequent performance degradation. This is the method that would be used by an organization that wants a simple, standard approach and is satisfied with the loading and performance considerations.

For a production application it is essential to use static SQL, and with good design the performance, data integrity and security are as high as when using a transaction-based approach.

Transaction access offers the highest potential both for network efficiency and for an optimal response time. It also offers a consistent solution to the access of mixed relational and non-relational data. However, it needs more programmer resources and more careful design than direct SQL does. Maintenance is more complex as it requires the management of both client and server modules, buffers, conversations, error handling, and extra tools and environments. This is the approach that would be taken by a technically sophisticated organization that wants high performance and can handle a complex solution. It requires good technical staff and the time to plan the best approach, and involves some danger that the solution will be non-standard.

PC Perspective

This section shows how the needs for PC data access have evolved over the last five years. The initial justification for PCs was based on productivity gains achieved using packages to perform certain business functions. Many departments and small businesses are run on a spreadsheet, a database, or both. This is fine until you reach the limits of the package and start using it for tasks it was not designed to perform – for example, the use of Lotus 1-2-3 to manipulate and report on large volumes of data records. Soon you will find that you are looking for another package and ways to convert your data from one package's format to another. This is possible and generally not too difficult, as most packages have an export/import facility.

The problem is – what happens when you change the data in one package and not the rest? Now you have data integrity and integration issues to worry about. It becomes clear that packages alone are not the total solution.

The problems become much greater when you introduce a mainframe or mid-range computer. The host systems do not support the same data types as the PCs and do not run the same packages, but information needs to be exchanged between PC and host applications as well as between PC users.

Just as there is a limit to PC packages, there is often an even greater limit to host applications. Most host applications are built to be either batch (process some input and produce a report) or on-line (read and write to a dumb screen).

The dumb screen and the 'package-running PC' can be combined by adding a communications board to the PC. We have come about as far as we can go in turning PCs into dumb screens. A PC can be made to act like any model of 3270 screen or printer, text or graphics, local or remote, and it can even be made to look like a 3174 controller if you wish.

However, using the extensive power of a PC to make it behave as a dumb terminal has obvious deficiencies in getting the best out of your computing resources. It is not only PCs that are capable of much more, but host applications as well.

Client/server applications are designed to get the best from both the PC and the host. Applications designed with a PC in mind benefit both the end-user because of their better user interface, and also the organization because of their higher productivity and the ability to support new types of applications. For example, applications can include consolidated information that is up-to-date and maintained on the host, and this can be linked to packages running on local workstations.

The missing ingredients have been a suitable PC platform and tools to implement the new breed of application capable of communicating in a transparent, structured, secure way with workstations, minis and mainframes.

Local area networks

The step following the stand-alone PC was a number of PCs connected by a local area network (LAN). Typically, one PC on this network contained the information that was shared by all the other PCs. This PC is the file server.

The major use of LANs today is to share disks, printers and communication facilities among a number of PCs. Most applications are much as they have been since 1984, with perhaps some e-mail and limited shared databases being the only additional use of the LAN environment.

Most so-called 'LAN versions' of PC packages are just the same old stand-alone PC applications, being loaded from a file server instead of a local hard disk. Many packages needed some cleaning up of sloppy code so that they could open and close files and printers properly to make them work in a LAN environment. Some also needed modifications to support more than just the A–C drives, as LAN drivers can be anywhere from A to Z. Apart from these 'cleaning up' changes, there is often some pricing advantage to the LAN version, but the applications nevertheless behave just as they do in stand-alone mode.

Networked applications

Once PCs were stand-alone, and applications were isolated. Each PC had its own database and users could only communicate by transferring files – a slow, laborious process that meant everyone's database was out of date.

With the advent of PC LANs, everyone used applications that accessed the same database. This is sometimes inappropriately described as a client/server approach, because every application is a client to the file server. However, this limited client/server approach has performance limitations which can only get worse with the growing amount of data being stored and shipped around LANs.

Consider a simple operation:

> Read through all the orders in an order entry database and display the total order value for customers in the Northern region.

This means sending the entire database across the LAN, record by record. The PC application checks each record to see if the customer is in the Northern region and, if so, adds the order value to a total. The process is very inefficient and very slow.

Despite the on-going battle to decide if a 10 megabit per second Ethernet is faster than a 16 megabit per second Token Ring network, it is usually the way in which the application processing is distributed that is the critical factor in measuring LAN performance.

Better ways to access data

There are smarter ways to do things. The problem is dealing with files, when applications should be working with data. What is needed is a way for the application to send a description of what data it actually needs. All the work can then be done at the other end, and just the result returned – a single number. This would be a very efficient use of the LAN and would mean that more PCs could be attached and more could be done.

But how can a description be sent? The answer is Structured Query Language (SQL). For example, the following SQL request performs the above operation:

    Select sum(value) from orders where region='North'

In this case the description is sent to the database server. The server scans the database locally, summing all the order values for customers in the Northern region, and then it sends the single number back to the PC. All the database processing is performed where it should be performed – on the server. If the database server runs out of steam, then this single machine can be upgraded to a more powerful one. New applications need to use SQL. Instead of writing for dumb terminals or squeezing the last ounce out of stand-alone packages in a multi-user environment, we should be looking to program them on the PC. In the past, this needed teams of system analysts producing a mammoth specification that was then implemented by large teams of programmers. This led to huge backlogs and a general jamming up of the works. The programming aids and tools were inadequate, and the communications capabilities were incomplete for application programmers to write client/server applications.

Well, times have changed. Before looking at development techniques in detail, we first need to think about the PC operating system.

Summary

The first aspect to consider when planning the implementation of client/server applications is how the data will be distributed and accessed. This chapter has described three basic sources of data and considered a number of ways to access them. The particular method and architecture used will determine the programming complexity, data integrity, performance and security of the final system. Each method was considered against a set of requirements and the advantages and disadvantages of each described.

Screen renovation is a 'quick and dirty' approach which provides a good way to get started but not a long-term solution.

All the major SQL databases now provide distributed data access. This enables PCs to access data in a deceptively simple way. To achieve the stated requirements, care must be taken in how the architecture is implemented. Without this care there will be problems of data integrity and application performance.

The third method covers a multitude of communications techniques under the heading 'transaction processing'. Whatever technique is used, it is important that the well-established requirements for data integrity and security are maintained. The easiest way to satisfy these requirements is to use a well-established transaction processing system, such as CICS. CICS can be easily accessed from a workstation and it is a good solution to the problem of accessing the 70% of corporate data that is not in SQL form.

Finally, many of the PC applications that have been developed use PC tools, and PC databases are inefficient for complex inquiries and do not hold the data in a form that is compatible with corporate mainframe standards. It is now time to transfer these applications to SQL databases using appropriate development tools.

CHAPTER 3

CLIENT OPERATING SYSTEMS

Your desktop is the battleground on which the biggest computer companies in the world are fighting for ownership. The companies that control this vital market will be those that control the corporate computer market in the future.

Their primary weapon is the operating system, or more precisely the programming interface to the operating system. This is because users buy applications, not operating systems, and applications must be written to use a particular programming interface. The operating system with most applications that most users want to buy will be the most successful. Success can be measured in terms of money invested in a particular company's proprietary programming interface.

The other battle taking place is over whose processor chip will be inside the desktop computer. However, if the operating system can isolate the applications from this choice, then ultimately no one controls this market as no investment has been made by the end-user. If the user can buy an Intel computer one day and a RISC-based computer the next without being aware of the difference, then market share becomes solely a matter of price/performance.

This book is not about the whole desktop computer market but about one important part – the high-end client/server market. This market has its own requirements and its own dynamics. It is an important market because, although it is smaller than the market for PCs to run personal productivity software, it involves a large corporate investment in associated hardware, support, development and infrastructure costs. Much of this investment is made in a particular operating system and is not easily moved to a different one. However, one important dynamic in the market is that development tools are becoming operating system-independent. This means that applications developed using these tools are not locked into a single operating system and so the investment is made in the application rather than the operating system.

Operating systems

We need to examine the workstation operating systems and how they match up to the requirements of a high-end client operating system (see Table 3.1). One fundamental assumption is that your organization has a large number of PC users with DOS and Windows applications running on Intel processors.

Notice that these requirements are very different from the requirements of an operating system to run personal productivity software.

The criteria rule out 16-bit DOS/Windows 3.1 because of the need for 32-bit operation, multi-tasking and a stable operating system. Windows 3.1 is a sophisticated graphical user interface on top of an unprotected, 16-bit operating system with no memory protection or multi-tasking capability and limited communications and database handling. It provides a good user interface but with nothing behind it to support corporate client/server applications. Microsoft has addressed these limitations by developing a new range of operating systems based on a 32-bit programming interface.

32-bit with memory protection

If you were to ask anyone whether operating systems will be 16-bit or 32-bit in two years, they would obviously say 32-bit. In addition, 32-bit operation allows applications to perform better as all new PCs have 32-bit hardware.

The justification for 16-bit is based on the wide range of DOS/Windows 3.1 products. However, there is now no need to compromise for client/server applications as there are 32-bit products for both OS/2 and Windows. If you are concerned about the extra memory that Windows NT requires, remember that

Table 3.1 Requirements for client operating systems.

1. An operating system that you will not need to replace within two years and which provides good performance and stability; this essentially means 32-bit with memory protection between programs

2. True multi-tasking

3. Good communications and database support, including easy access to mainframe and mid-range computers

4. Ability to run DOS and Windows personal productivity applications efficiently

5. Efficient Intel implementation

your client/server applications are likely to be in use for many years, so make decisions that address the future. Alternatively, you can either start now using OS/2 or wait until Windows 95 becomes generally available. The availability and hardware demands of each of these choices are discussed in detail later in this chapter.

The other aspect of this requirement is memory protection. Without proper memory management, one application is able to overwrite the memory space of another. This means that the correctness of the data can never be guaranteed. In addition, an incorrect memory access can crash the complete system, necessitating a reboot and lengthy delays. Windows 95, Windows NT and OS/2 provide full memory protection between processes.

Do not be misled by the ability of Windows 3.1 to run 32-bit applications that conform to the Win32s specification (described later) as this does not provide full memory protection or multi-tasking. Although the applications are 32-bit, the operating system is still the same 16-bit code running on DOS.

True multi-tasking

The need for multi-tasking is also particular to client/server applications. As the objective is to make the user more responsive, it is important that avoidable delays are prevented. For example, if a lengthy mainframe data access process is initiated, the user should not have to wait, say, 30 seconds for it to complete before being able to continue.

Multi-tasking changes the way users interact with the system. Multi-tasking applications need to be designed that way from the start. You cannot just bolt it on later, because it changes the way the user can interact with the system. You need to make the decision today that is right for the application, now and for the future. Again, true pre-emptive multi-tasking is available with Windows NT, Windows 95 and OS/2.

Good mainframe connectivity

As the client operating system needs to access data from the corporate data server (see Chapter 2) this requires suitable connectivity products to be available. There is a wide range of connectivity products available for OS/2 because it has been available for some years and IBM has been committed to linking OS/2 into its mainframe environment.

A limited number of 32-bit Windows products are currently available, but many more are expected to be released during 1995.

Runs DOS/Windows applications well

There are tens of millions of users of DOS and Windows applications, and tens of thousands of applications available. All the major personal productivity applications are available under DOS and Windows. It is therefore important that the client operating system should be able to run most of these applications and run them efficiently. OS/2 and Windows 95 run a wide range of DOS and 16-bit Windows applications but there are some restrictions imposed by Windows NT because of its strict hardware protection.

Efficient Intel implementation

The story of the next-generation operating system for the Intel chip started on 2 April 1987 when IBM and Microsoft jointly announced OS/2 as the replacement for DOS and Windows. This operating system was promoted as the standard for the future.

However, the spectacular success of the launch of Windows 3.0 in May 1990 caused Microsoft to drop support for OS/2 and switch all of its resources to Windows. Meanwhile, IBM had become totally committed to the success of OS/2 as part of its overall direction.

The two companies immediately started a battle for the desktop that is still going on today. Microsoft had an early lead which quickly grew into an enormous market share. IBM had a strong position in the corporate marketplace and established OS/2 in many key sites where a sturdy operating system was needed for client/server applications.

The original OS/2 operating system was 16-bit and only ran one single DOS application at a time. However, it provided multi-tasking and protection against program crashes, and the 'Extended Edition' version provided an SQL database and mainframe connectivity. OS/2 therefore started to be used for building corporate applications with a PC front-end and a mainframe back-end – in other words, client/server applications.

More than one million copies of the OS/2 1.x series were sold. Sales of Windows 3 dwarfed this figure within a few months of its launch, but the total investment associated with each OS/2 sale was substantially greater. This investment took the form of large projects involving development, support, infrastructure and hardware costs.

During 1992 an entirely new version of OS/2 was launched, called OS/2 2.0. The OS/2 2.x series was a major advance over the 1.x series. It ran multiple DOS and Windows applications, it was 32 bit and had a new user interface. In addition, IBM offered a wide range of connectivity products that made it suitable for client/server applications.

Windows is now established as the standard graphical user interface for DOS with over 60 million units shipped. OS/2 is used for corporate client/server applications and for high-end client use, with approximately 6 million units shipped.

With the turmoil, uncertainty and battles in the marketplace over the last few years, it might be thought that the operating system issues are now all settled and the choices clear. However life is never that simple. A new round of upheaval is about to start. The reason is best illustrated with a diagram (see Figure 3.1).

The hatched areas represent operating systems that are not currently shipping. It can be seen that there are not two operating systems to consider but six. If this is limited to 32-bit operating systems then there are two currently on general release – OS/2 Warp 3.0 and Windows NT 3.5 – and two that should become available soon – Workplace OS and Windows 95. Let us now look at the IBM operating systems first followed by the Microsoft offerings.

OS/2

OS/2 is a single-user, multi-tasking operating system capable of running multiple applications and communicating with many other machines – with none of the compromises so very necessary under DOS/Windows 3.1.

Since its launch in 1988, OS/2 has been used primarily to run applications that

	IBM	Microsoft
Server and high-end workstation	Workplace OS	Windows NT
32-bit workstation	OS/2 Warp	Windows 95
16-bit PC	OS/2 1.x	Windows 3.1

Figure 3.1 Client operating systems.

access corporate data, although this is now changing. IBM claimed in 1992 that over $4 billion was committed to corporate applications being developed under OS/2.

There have been seven major releases of OS/2:

- 1988 OS/2 1.0 – the original 16-bit character-based version.

- 1989 OS/2 1.1 – the first version with a GUI, called Presentation Manager.

- 1990 OS/2 1.2 – a functionally extended version.

- 1991 OS/2 1.3 – a smaller-size, higher-performance version with further increased functionality.

- 1992 OS/2 2.0 – a 32-bit version with a new user interface called the Workplace Shell. It ran multiple DOS, Windows 3.0 and OS/2 16-bit and 32-bit applications.

- 1993 OS/2 2.1 – an updated version with support for Windows 3.1 applications, true type fonts, 32-bit seamless high-resolution display drivers, additional printer support, laptop/notebook power management and PCMCIA support, additional SCSI and CD-ROM drivers and multimedia support. This version is also available as a product called 'OS/2 for Windows', which installs on top of DOS/Windows and is available at low cost.

- 1994 OS/2 Warp – a new high performance version with 32-bit graphics, the ability to run in a 4-megabyte machine and many bundled applications. This version will take OS/2 into the home and small business markets and so spread the base of users.

The old OS/2 1.x series could be bought as either Standard Edition (OS/2 only) or Extended Edition (OS/2 with communications facilities and a database called Database Manager). With the OS/2 2.x series, Extended Edition was unbundled into separate products – OS/2 and Extended Services. The two products in Extended Services can now be bought individually as Communications Manager/2 and DB2/2 (a new product compatible with the old OS/2 Database Manager database).

OS/2 Warp

'OS/2 Warp is as easy to use as the Mac, runs multiple DOS and Windows programs efficiently, fully exploits the power of the processor and is stable enough to run corporate applications.'

This is a summary of OS/2. Let us examine each part of this statement in turn:

- 'as easy to use as the Mac' – OS/2 has a user interface called the Workplace Shell. This object-oriented user interface provides features similar to those of the Apple Macintosh. The user can create folders that contain spreadsheets, documents, graphics or other folders. A document is edited by double clicking on it. Underneath this interface are the old-style directory structures required by DOS and Windows programs.

- 'runs multiple DOS and Windows programs efficiently' – OS/2 makes more memory available to DOS programs than does DOS 6 and it provides a high-performance version of FAT (the DOS and Windows filing system).

- 'fully exploits the power of the processor' – OS/2 is a full 32-bit operating system and therefore can exploit the full power of the PCs on which it runs.

- 'stable enough to run corporate applications' – OS/2 prevents any single program from crashing the machine, and also runs multiple applications efficiently with thread support and pre-emptive multi-tasking.

OS/2's DOS and Windows support

DOS was designed for use as a single-tasking, single-user environment. It was designed for a now out-of-date processor (8088) with memory adequate for a single user doing one thing at a time.

DOS works perfectly well on a stand-alone PC running DOS packages, or a LAN-based PC using shared resources, or communicating as a dumb screen to a mainframe. However, its client/server capabilities are almost non-existent.

The ability of OS/2 to run DOS comes from exploiting a feature of the 386 chip – it is able to run many 'virtual' machines. Each machine is like a separate conventional PC, that is how OS/2 can run multiple DOS applications with such good performance.

What does all this mean to the DOS and 16-bit Windows user? In summary OS/2 will:

- Run multiple DOS applications and allow the user to switch between them. These applications can use the same DOS device drivers that they have always used.

- Run multiple versions of DOS at the same time.

- Make about 640 000 bytes of memory available to the application.

- Increase the maximum extended memory from 16 megabytes to 48 megabytes.

- Run DOS graphics in a window; for example, two business graphics applications can be plotting in two windows on the same screen at the same time.

- Provide a much faster filing system that is compatible with the current DOS filing system.

- Stop one application from over-writing another. With DOS any application that corrupts the operating system requires the computer to be rebooted, if and when it is detected. OS/2 localizes the damage to that single application. Other applications can continue running and the machine does not need to be rebooted.

- Handle swapping more effectively than Windows 3.1. Windows 3.1 users have found that to run a number of Windows applications at the same time and switch between them quickly requires 8 megabytes of physical memory. When more memory is needed, both Windows and OS/2 can swap parts of memory out to disk to use the freed memory. OS/2 does this very efficiently and, unlike Windows, dynamically uses and frees space.

- Allow multiple DOS applications to print concurrently – OS/2 has a print spooler that provides correct spooling of printer output for all applications, including concurrent DOS applications.

- Run DOS applications that handle hardware devices directly and are very time-sensitive. With Windows, these applications must run in the foreground and all other applications must be suspended. OS/2 allows multiple time-critical, hardware-dependent applications to run in both the foreground and background.

OS/2's distributed architecture

OS/2 is an important part of a number of key IBM software technologies and architectures. These include SystemView (the system management strategy), NetView (a host-based network management system), LAN NetView (an OS/2-based network management system), DRDA (the Distributed Relational Database Architecture supported by all the major IBM operating systems, including OS/2, AS/400, AIX and MVS), CICS (a transaction processing system for OS/2, AS/400, AIX and MVS), CID (Configuration, Installation and Distribution products) and LANfocus Management/2 (an OS/2-based set of tools for distributed system management).

The products available within each of these families are in turn based on industry standards. For example, for distributed system management they are based on three standards:

- The International Standards Organisation (ISO) Open System Interconnect (OSI) X.700 family of standards.

- The Open Software Foundation (OSF) and X-OPEN standards for the Distributed Management Environment (DME) and Distributed Computing Environment (DCE).

- The Simple Network Management Protocol (SNMP) defined by the Internet Architecture Board.

The selection of products discussed in the sections below indicate the extent of the options available with OS/2.

LAN Server

In order to provide server services, a subsystem called LAN Server needs to be run on top of OS/2. This compares with Novell's NetWare which is a complete, dedicated server operating system.

Novell's NetWare is a high-performance file server that supports a large number of PC users running personal productivity software. It provides a basic file and resource-sharing capability. However, client/server applications require a database server running on a general-purpose operating system capable of running gateways, control systems, application components and batch jobs. OS/2 with LAN Server is ideal in this role as it provides a consistent solution for both the client and the server.

With the growth in client/server applications (which manipulate data) the days of the dedicated file server must be limited. Files are a low-level concept introduced for the benefit of computers. Even word-processor users do not really want to invent eight-character names (which mean that they will never be able to find their documents again.)

Communications Manager

Communications Manager/2 provides 3270, asynchronous and APPC (Advanced Program to Program Communications) support, and other features such as 5250 and host gateway support.

DB2/2

DB2/2 provides a 32-bit relational database based on DB2, with SQL being the standard access language. DB2/2 integrity support includes forward recovery, logging of system errors, implicit row-level lock, explicit table lock and deadlock detection.

DDCS/2

DDCS/2 (Distributed Database Connection Services/2) allows an OS/2 application to transparently access any combination of DB2/2, DB2 or SQL/DS on a mainframe, SQL/400 on an AS/400, or DB2/6000 on an RS/6000.

CICS

CICS OS/2 Version 2 provides both a LAN-based high-performance transaction processing environment and direct access to CICS mainframe data and applications. The CICS family now runs on the AS/400, RS/6000 and other UNIX machines, as well as the IBM mainframe operating systems. It is currently the dominant transaction processing standard and its market share is forecast to grow.

OS/2 System Object Model (SOM)

In October 1991, IBM and Apple announced the formation of a new software company subsequently named Taligent. Taligent's Chief Executive Officer, Joe Guglielmi, stated in their corporate brochure that 'the full exploitation of object technology has the potential – like other breakthrough technologies such as the transistor, magnetic media and the microprocessor – to drive major paradigm shifts and fuel new periods of expansive growth and innovation'.

Unfortunately for Taligent, the last thing the computer world wants at the moment is another operating system. For any new operating system to succeed, it needs software vendors to invest in writing application software, but the software community will only do this if the operating system gives them a new market of substantial size. The only way in which this 'chicken and egg' dilemma can be resolved is backward compatibility. If a new operating system can run existing applications better than before, users will switch to it, a market will exist, software developers will write applications and the operating system has a chance of long-term success.

The question is, therefore, how can all of Taligent's good work be brought to market? The answer proposed by IBM and Taligent is to incorporate it gradually into an existing operating system without losing backward compatibility. And the operating system in question? – OS/2.

IBM has already developed a sophisticated object-oriented subsystem for OS/2 called the System Object Model, or SOM (pronounced 'som'). SOM is used to implement the new user interface, called the Workplace Shell. SOM handles messages passed between objects written in different languages. It enables new objects and their relationship with existing objects to be defined. It can be used by OS/2 developers to enable them to build language-independent objects.

Over the next two years IBM will be launching a series of increasingly powerful object support features. The first is Distributed SOM, or DSOM (pronounced 'dee som'). This enables an object on one system to communicate transparently with an object on another system. This communication will follow the CORBA (Common Object Request Broker Architecture) standard agreed to by the OMG (Object Management Group). DSOM will also use the DCE (Distributed Computing Environment) standard allowing interoperability with most major operating systems. Following this will be 'frameworks' derived from the development at Taligent. A framework is a set of related objects, what would normally be called a library or a subsystem.

If Taligent could then release an object-oriented operating system that ran all existing applications, and ran them better, it could succeed in the market. This new operating system could be launched on top of IBM's Workplace OS (see below).

OS/2 future directions

There are now many OS/2 add-on products being released by IBM. Multimedia PM/2 is now shipping with OS/2 Warp. The Distributed System Object Model (DSOM), DCE (Distributed Computing Environment) support, Pen PM and Symmetric Multi-Processing (SMP) support are all now available.

OS/2 Warp is an important upgrade to Version 2.1. It incorporates many applications including a spreadsheet, word processor, fax support, diary and Internet access. It has 'single button' install and many more device drivers. There is a corporate client version that includes network support and improved systems management.

Workplace OS

Workplace OS is IBM's cross-platform version of OS/2. Strictly speaking, it is the name of a microkernel that will run on Intel and RISC processors and support a number of different operating systems. One of these operating systems will be OS/2.

A microkernel is a small software library that the operating system uses, rather than use the hardware directly. The benefit of this is that the operating system can be ported to new hardware more easily. The disadvantage is that it is less efficient to use a simulated architecture rather than exploit the particular machine's hardware architecture directly. The skill is in developing a microkernel that efficiently maps on to all the current hardware architectures.

UNIX, Workplace OS and Windows NT are all based on the Mach (pronounced 'mark') microkernel technology created at Carnegie Mellon University.

The Workplace OS microkernel is general enough to enable different operating systems to be run on top of it. IBM is describing this as the ability to run different 'personalities' on the same desktop. A personality is an operating system and so far Workplace OS is destined to support OS/2, DOS/Windows, UNIX (AIX, AUX and COSE versions) and Mac System 7. Workplace OS enables all these operating systems (or any subset) to run on the same machine at the same time and it enables the user to switch between them. There will be one main operating system (called the dominant personality) which defines the desktop.

Whether multiple simultaneous operating systems is a feature that anyone wants or needs is a largely irrelevant question because the main purpose of Workplace OS is to run operating systems on IBM's new RISC processor – the Power PC. Workplace OS will support the Power PC version of OS/2. This will add C2 security and symmetric multi-processing (SMP). SMP support is important for high-performance database servers running on multi-processor machines. It enables the various tasks in the system to run on all the processors at the same time. SMP support is also available for OS/2 as an installable library.

Windows

Microsoft announced their plans to launch Windows in October 1983, and in November 1985 they began shipping Windows 1.0. There were few applications available for this first version and its hardware requirements stretched the hardware of the day to the limit.

Microsoft and IBM jointly announced their plans to develop OS/2 in April 1987 and the first version started shipping in late 1987. However, Microsoft continued their Windows development and in 1988 a version for the Intel 80386 was launched and Windows version 2.0 started to sell. Developers began to write applications and Windows version 3.0 was under active development.

Finally, after five years and over $100 million spent on development, Microsoft launched Windows version 3.0 on 22 May 1990. It quickly became a success and sold one million copies in the first four months.

Microsoft's Windows 3.1 has now shipped over 60 million copies and runs on most PCs capable of supporting a graphical user interface. It ships pre-installed on 78% of all new PCs and most of the major applications are available in Windows versions.

Windows 3.1's future is limited, however – it uses a 16-bit programming interface and Microsoft plans to move all software to their new 32-bit programming interface, called Win32.

This new interface has been criticized because it comes in many forms – Win32, supported by Windows NT only, Win32s ('s' for subset), supported by both Windows 3.1 and Windows NT, and Win32c, supported by the Windows 95 operating system. Figure 3.2 shows that Win32s is a small subset of Win32.

Most software vendors have stated that they intend to support Windows NT by converting their Win16 applications to Win32s. As Win32s is supported by both Windows 3.1 and Windows NT, the vendors can then sell a single product that runs under both operating systems. However, as Figure 3.2 indicates, the Win32s world is a small part of the world of Win32, since it exploits only a part of the functionality of Win32.

This means that customers will be buying 32-bit products for 32-bit Windows that are simply 16-bit products in disguise. In order to exploit the features of Win32 that are required for client/server applications (including aspects as fundamental as multi-tasking), software vendors must completely re-engineer their products.

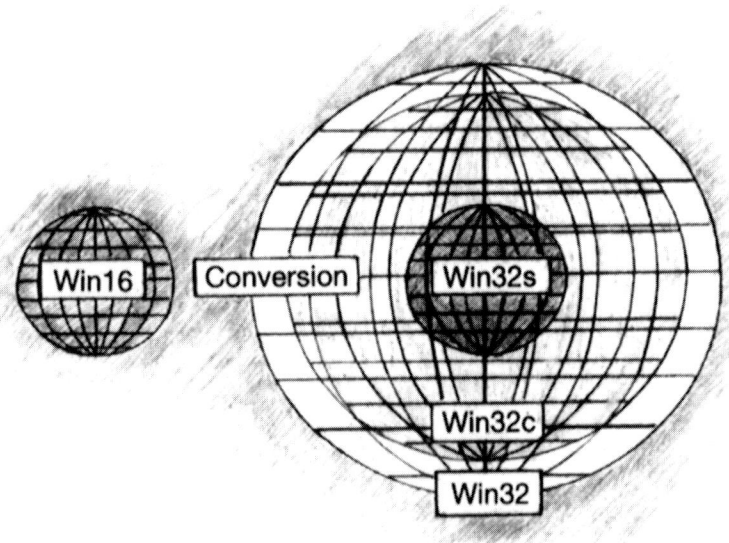

Figure 3.2 The Windows API worlds.

32-Bit Windows

Windows NT is the first 32-bit, true multi-tasking operating system that runs DOS, 16-bit Windows and a new generation of 32-bit Windows applications written to the Win32 programming interface. The 'NT' stands for New Technology; Windows NT is an entirely new operating system built from the ground up. It was started in October 1988 by David Cutler, formerly the architect of the DEC VAX/VMS operating system. It went into pre-release production in July 1992 and started shipping in August 1993. It has a microkernel architecture, portability, threaded symmetric multi-processing and C2 security.

NT comes in two forms – Windows NT Workstation and Windows NT Server. Both versions have built-in networking capabilities, but the Server version has the full set of LAN Manager 2.2 features, including fault tolerance, with the addition of drive duplexing, disk mirroring and centralized network administration and management.

NT takes Microsoft into many new markets. DOS/Windows is a limited, Intel-only operating system for PCs. NT could run on virtually any computer and provide all the features of the most advanced operating systems available.

As examples of new markets for Microsoft, NT will run on the latest generation of RISC processors, support the most advanced multi-processing hardware for computationally intensive applications, is suitable as a server, scalable from small Intel processors to mainframe-power multi-processor RISC machines, and provides the desktop features for client/server applications.

As a server, NT's main strength is that it is scalable. At the moment there are two types of servers – PC servers running either Novell's NetWare or OS/2, and mid-range RISC machines running UNIX. It is difficult to upgrade from one environment to the other. NT is a single solution for both types of servers. Workplace OS will provide the same scalability for OS/2 when it is released in 1995.

Also important is NT's ability to exploit the power of the next generation of hardware products. Even today there are very powerful multi-processor PC servers available with eight processors, 64 megabytes of main storage and multiple gigabyte drives.

However, the most important aspect of Windows NT in the context of this book is that it satisfies all the criteria given earlier for a client operating system. Its disadvantage is that it requires an Intel 486 with 16 megabytes of memory.

The resources required by NT are often referred to in the PC press as a justification for their claims that NT will not succeed on the desktop PC. It is true that NT is not a direct replacement for Windows 3.1, but criticizing NT for this is a short-sighted view. A more valid comparison is between NT and UNIX on the desktop. IDC forecasts 2.4 million UNIX systems on the desktop by 1996, yet UNIX is a more resource-hungry operating system than NT and also does not run DOS or Windows applications. UNIX has weak control of the desktop market, so it seems more likely that NT will take the market away from it. Although 2.4 million units may be a much lower number than that which Windows 3.1 achieved, nevertheless it is a new market and a key strategic one, as it determines the direction in which corporations will go over the next ten years.

NT on the desktop is also a stepping stone towards Windows 95 being the successor to Windows 3.1.

Windows NT comprises the Executive, which is the kernel that handles all the basic operating system functions and supports a User mode that runs the protected subsystems in which applications run. The Executive runs on top of a hardware abstraction layer (HAL), which provides a common interface on different platforms – Intel, DEC Alpha and MIPS – while hiding platform differences. Some 98% of NT is written in C/C++, so to run on different platforms the source code is recompiled and run on the hardware-specific HAL. Applications need only be recompiled for each platform; typically no other changes are required.

Windows Open Systems Architecture (WOSA)

WOSA is Microsoft's outline for defining how Windows can become a universal client that can fit seamlessly into a variety of different ('heterogeneous' in the jargon) corporate computing environments.

WOSA is a commitment by Microsoft to define, publish and comply with a range of programming interfaces for back-end services such as mail, directory, database connectivity, communications, interoperability and software licensing.

By defining a standard programming interface, products can access facilities provided by a range of 'service providers'. Corporate users can network their PCs and choose applications without being locked into a set of services determined by their previous decisions.

For example, if all application development tools use the WOSA ODBC (Open Database Connectivity) specification for database access, and if all database providers conform to ODBC, then applications can be developed independently of the database used.

Thus front-end desktop applications use WOSA to access mail, databases and other back-end services, and the back-end systems make their services available to the front-end applications through WOSA.

Important WOSA specifications are ODBC for data access, MAPI (Messaging Application Programming Interface), the License Service API and the Win32 API for file and print services.

WOSA will specifically target environments such as SNA, DEC's Network Applications Support (NAS), Novell's NetWare and Distributed Computing Environment (DCE).

ODBC

The ODBC API was announced in November 1991. It is a vendor-independent standard based on the Call Level Interface (CLI) specification developed by the SQL Access Group, a consortium of leading hardware and software database vendors.

In 1992 IBM, Borland and others jointly announced an alternative standard called IDAPI.

The success of each standard will depend on their use by both front-end tools and service providers, and their ability to do the job. If important services are omitted from the standard, then front-end tools will write directly to the back-end service providers. It should be noted that the front-end suppliers are already motivated to insulate the user from the back-end service providers. The WOSA standards potentially make that task easier and more complete.

ODBC supports the following features:

- A library of function calls that allow an application to establish a connection with a database, execute SQL (and non-SQL) statements and retrieve results.

- A subset of standard X/Open SQL grammar for accessing data.

- Non-standard database features: the application can check with the driver to see if a feature is available before issuing a request.

- Standardized encoding formats for SQL data and error codes.

Windows object linking and embedding (OLE)

Object linking and embedding (OLE 2.0) is a set of services that provide a powerful means for the user to build new objects from existing objects. Under the covers, OLE 2.0 is an application programming interface (API) that defines a set of functions programmers can use to incorporate advanced object linking and embedding capabilities into their applications. OLE 2.0 is also a set of services that will be built into future versions of the Windows operating system to support the API.

OLE is usually described as a means of creating documents consisting of multiple sources of information from different applications. Objects can be almost any type of information, including text, bitmap images, vector graphics, and even voice annotation and video clips.

OLE 2.0 is more than just a set of new features to implement within applications. It is the foundation of a new model of computing that will appear in future versions of the Windows operating system. All future versions of Windows will build upon OLE 2.0 to offer a more intuitive user interface and a distributed object computing model that extends the power of objects to networks while hiding the complexity of network environments.

Windows future directions

Microsoft's vision of 'Windows everywhere' is being realized by a growing family of related products. These include Windows for Workgroups, Windows for Pens, Mobile Windows (adds portable computing features), WinPad (for hand-held PCs and PDAs) and Modular Windows (inside home automation systems, fax machines and copiers).

The most significant new version for client/server applications is Windows 95.

Windows 95

Windows 95 (previously referred to as 'Chicago') is the replacement to DOS/Windows 3.1 and will be the first direct competitor to OS/2. Details of Windows 95 have appeared in the press and been described in the *Microsoft System Journal*. Windows 95 is a 32-bit, true multi-tasking operating system with a new object-oriented graphical user interface and, although Windows 95 does not support all of the Windows NT programming interface, it is easy to write a program that will run on both.

The most likely date for general availability is mid-1995. Figure 3.1 shows that by the end of 1995 Windows NT will be positioned against Workplace OS, as server and high-end client operating systems, and Windows 95 will be positioned against OS/2 as a client operating system.

Windows 95 is a major new operating system. Although it still incorporates

DOS it has a full 32-bit core. In many ways Windows 95 is surprisingly similar to OS/2. Like OS/2 (and unlike NT), Windows 95 virtualizes all device access for 16-bit DOS and Windows applications, so the vast majority of existing applications will still work – even most low-level disk utilities. It has an object-oriented user interface that is very like OS/2's Workplace Shell, even down to the settings or properties notebooks; also, like OS/2, Windows 95 is optimized for the Intel architecture and is not portable to RISC machines.

Windows versus OS/2

Comparison of Windows and OS/2 is difficult as both operating systems are evolving. Windows NT should be compared with Workplace OS, and Windows 95 with OS/2 Warp. Because of these difficulties I have chosen to compare the two 32-bit operating systems that are currently shipping in mid-1994 – OS/2 2.1 and Windows NT version 3.1 – and have noted future product features to avoid a misleading comparison.

This difficulty of comparing OS/2 and Windows will not become easier over time because they will jump ahead of each other with each new release. However, some common themes can be seen – by 1995 both families of operating system will be 32-bit, multi-tasking, have RISC versions, run DOS and Windows applications, and have good connectivity and efficient Intel implementations.

The choice of operating system then becomes difficult to make on a feature basis. As suppliers, IBM and Microsoft come from different backgrounds. IBM offers good integration with their mainframe systems and the early availability of these products under OS/2 (for example, DB2/2 and CICS for OS/2). Microsoft dominates both the PC applications software and operating system markets.

It is interesting that both companies are stressing the opposite in their marketing literature. IBM is presenting itself as a technology company based on its lead with object-orientation, SOM and its partnership with Taligent, while Microsoft presents itself as having the best system solution, based on its mainframe connectivity and wide area network management.

If we compare Windows and OS/2 as at mid-1994, both Windows NT and OS/2 provide a robust platform for client/server development. They have memory protection to prevent rogue processes bringing down the system or from interfering with other processes, pre-emptive multi-tasking to run the many threads and processes necessary to access networks, communications lines and databases simultaneously, and sophisticated graphical interfaces to allow easy access to data. They both run DOS and 16-bit Windows applications (to a greater or lesser extent) and are 32-bit to exploit today's hardware fully. OS/2 is well established and provides excellent support for legacy applications.

All these similarities must be remembered when looking at the differences between the two systems.

Backward compatibility

OS/2 will run DOS device drivers, DOS applications (that do not use 32-bit protected mode instructions), Windows 2, Windows 3, OS/2 16-bit and OS/2 32-bit applications.

Windows NT will run DOS applications (that do not access the hardware directly), Windows 3, Windows NT, OS/2 and POSIX (a limited character-based UNIX) applications. NT's OS/2 support is currently limited to 16-bit and 32-bit character-mode.

In order to provide C2 security, Windows NT prevents any application from writing directly to the hardware. This means that all-new device drivers are required, even to write to the built-in speaker. A number of Windows and DOS applications do not work because they try to access the hardware directly (for example, LapLink, SuperPrint, Windows 3.1 and WordPerfect printer drivers, certain parts of Norton Utilities and PC Tools, applications that require serial or parallel port access, or Windows 3.1 Enhanced mode VxD drivers). Adobe Type Manager also does not work, because it uses unsupported Windows 3.1 calls. DOS and Windows multimedia programs and DOS games are also likely to cause problems as they often access the hardware directly.

When NT runs on a RISC machine it is able to run existing DOS/Windows Intel binaries. It achieves this by software emulation of the Intel 286 hardware. On a powerful RISC processor this runs such applications at about the speed of a slow 386 machine.

If it is important to run a wide range of existing Windows 3.1 and DOS applications or any existing device drivers, OS/2 is the better choice. This OS/2 advantage is likely to disappear with Windows 95 as it uses a similar mechanism to achieve backward compatibility to OS/2.

Application Programmer's Interface (API)

The OS/2 PM API is widely considered to be superior to the Windows API, being more consistent and better designed. However, more applications have been written to the Windows 3 API than to the PM API, and most of these are likely to move to NT, as the graphical component of NT is basically Windows 3 converted to 32 bits.

Windows 95 supports a substantial subset of the Windows NT API but initially most vendors are likely to write applications for a much smaller subset (Win32s) so that they are still compatible with DOS/Windows 3.1. To encourage vendors to write to the full 32-bit, multi-tasking Windows 95 API, Microsoft has introduced a Windows 95 loop program that makes this a mandatory requirement.

Databases

IBM's strategic database for OS/2 is DB2/2. DB2 has a track record of running mission-critical applications on the mainframe, and it is now available on the PC. IBM have announced their intention to port DB2/2 to Windows NT but have indicated this may not be until 1995 at the earliest. IBM supports direct access from OS/2 to all their relational databases, using the DDCS/2 product.

Microsoft offers SQL/Server, a highly respected database engine from Sybase, under Windows NT. Microsoft has defined a common API, called ODBC, for all database access. All applications and tools that provide ODBC will access all databases that support it. At the time of writing, ODBC does not provide support for static SQL with IBM databases, a serious omission for production applications.

Many third party databases, such as Oracle, will also run on both platforms.

Hardware

Neither OS/2 nor DOS/Windows are practical on anything less than a 386SX, so DOS will continue as the standard for all the 286 machines already installed.

A basic OS/2 client machine is a 25 MHz 386 with 8 megabytes of memory, if running NetWare, and 12 megabytes of memory if running LAN Server requester. A basic Windows NT machine is a 33 MHz 486, with 16 megabytes of memory. OS/2 with network client software takes about 45 megabytes of disk space and NT takes about 80 megabytes. These figures refer to a basic client workstation – not the minimum required to run the operating system, which is in practice unusable.

Also they do not represent the requirements for a loaded system, such as a developer's workstation or a client workstation running multiple applications. In a client/server environment many users will want to be running many different applications at the same time. Most users will need or will find it convenient to have six or more programs running, for example, communications, a database, LAN requester, a word processor, a spreadsheet and multiple application programs. In these situations OS/2 will require 16 megabytes and Windows NT will require 24 megabytes of memory.

OS/2 requires about 20 to 30 megabytes of disk space, depending on the options selected, plus another 15 megabytes of swap file space. This does not include disk space for LAN, communications or database access. A typical OS/2 machine should have a minimum of about 120 megabytes of disk space. Also, remember that many new personal productivity tools now require at least 10 megabytes of disk space each, so the practical requirement could easily be a lot higher.

The recommended graphics standards for OS/2 and Windows NT is VGA or Super VGA. They also both support higher resolution standards, such as XGA. High-resolution screens offers about four times the apparent area of a VGA screen. As the user starts to control more and more applications, the need for this become more significant.

Windows NT requires more disk space for the base operating system and for its swap file. The practical minimum disk size is therefore about 200 megabytes.

Notice that the practical minimum specification machine for Windows NT is the high-specification machine for OS/2. The relative difference between the OS/2 and Window NT hardware requirements is similar to that which used to exist between 16-bit Windows and OS/2.

Windows 95 is designed to run in a 4-megabyte machine but as 8 megabytes is recommended by most users as the practical minimum for DOS/Windows 3.1, then 4 megabytes is likely to be the same theoretical minimum as claimed for OS/2.

IBM and Microsoft have said that future versions of OS/2 and Windows will have a lower memory requirement but, as there is a trade-off between memory usage and functionality, operating systems tend to grow and it is falling memory prices that eventually remove the concern.

Host communication

OS/2 has superior connectivity to other IBM platforms, and this seems likely to be true for a long while. OS/2 has terminal emulation products for renovating host-based applications, APPC for cooperative processing, DDCS/2 for direct connection to DB2 and CICS for OS/2.

Windows NT has products for terminal emulation and APPC and IBM CICS is available early in 1995 but no dates are available for DDCS/2 and DB2.

Multi-user

NT is a 'serial multi-user' operating system, that is, accounts for multiple users can be set up on one machine but only one user will use the machine at a time. It is possible for extra users to log in, for example, over serial lines, but this is only available in the Server version. Only one user can run graphical applications.

Networking

All versions of NT come with peer-to-peer networking built-in. However, almost all NT installations will still require a full-blooded server. The peer networking features in NT are comparable to Windows for Workgroups, while the Server provides LAN Manager style performance and administrative tools.

IBM already provides peer networking as part of its LAN Server 3.0 product, and will continue to enhance LAN Server. IBM's strategic direction is to continue to enhance LAN Server and the DCE product, allowing OS/2 servers to participate as peers in an open, distributed network. Both platforms have good NetWare connectivity, and Novell's market share will force them to keep up development in this area.

Open systems

IBM has a Distributed Computing Environment (DCE) product for OS/2 in beta testing at the time of writing. DCE is a complete environment for creating and managing distributed systems, supported by almost every major vendor, and it will allow heterogeneous systems to work together with unprecedented transparency. This is a new technology, but IBM's commitment to it is clear. In contrast, Microsoft is currently only providing the RPC (remote procedure call) component of DCE for NT, which will give none of the benefits of centralized management and security that DCE provides.

Both vendors have TCP/IP packages, although Microsoft's is less complete as it omits NFS (network file system – it makes remote file systems appear to be part of the local file system). Windows supports TCP/IP through the WinSockets interface.

NT has a POSIX subsystem. POSIX is a character-mode standard for UNIX applications, so UNIX applications written to this standard will run under NT. The main reason for this subsystem seems to have been to allow NT to comply with US Government Department of Defense directives that mandate POSIX compliance.

Security

NT is built to C2 security levels. The security features are likely to be significant only in the Server version of NT. At the workstation level, the security features combine with the multi-user features of NT to allow network administrators to set up files which end-users will be unable to change. Windows 95 does not provide C2 security.

IBM's approach to security is to enhance server products such as DCE and LAN Server rather than the client operating system, but IBM has said C2-level security will be added to a future version of OS/2.

Symmetric multi-processing (SMP)

NT will run on multi-processor machines, and take full advantage of the extra horsepower available. At the workstation level, multi-processor machines will speed up computationally expensive tasks such as 3-D graphics and desktop video. This does not seem very relevant to commercial users now, and will require new software to be written, but future user interfaces are likely to require ever higher amounts of processor power, and symmetric multi-processing is the cheapest way to get it. At the server level, multi-processor machines can speed up database servers dramatically. This is why database server vendors such as Sequent are investing in NT. SMP has almost no effect on the performance of file servers, as these tend to depend on the speed of their disks and network peripherals. Windows 95 is not likely to support SMP.

IBM provides an SMP version of OS/2 and the OS/2 development team is working with the DB2/2 team to ensure that the performance benefits are realized in the database. The Workplace OS microkernel will also support SMP.

User interface

NT has the same user interface as Windows 3, which is either a blessing (most users will not need substantial retraining) or a curse (NT deserves a better front-end). Most OS/2 users look on the Windows 3 user interface as cumbersome and rather primitive. OS/2 has a state-of-the-art user interface, with unified program and file managers, which Microsoft will provide in Windows 95 and the next major version of NT (codenamed 'Cairo').

Summary

Both families of operating system provide, or will be providing, very similar functionality on both the server and the client platforms. One difference is timing, as at the end of 1994 NT supports SMP, which will provide much better performance for database servers, and it runs on RISC chips, for users who demand the highest level of performance.

OS/2 is an excellent, tried and tested, all-purpose desktop client and server. It excels at connectivity and it already provides matchless connectivity to IBM hosts. The DCE product will open up the world of open, distributed systems. OS/2 has a superior user interface, and will run on much lower specification machines. It also has the benefit of being widely available and having a substantial installed user base (approximately 6 million).

When generally available, Windows 95 will provide all of the benefits of OS/2 to a prospective user community of 60 million people.

Other desktop operating systems

There are a small number of other graphical operating systems used on the desktop. The most important of these are a variety of UNIX operating systems and the Apple Mac System 7. In addition it is worth mentioning NeXTSTEP as probably the most advanced operating system currently available. NeXTSTEP illustrates the marketing problem for any new operating system – having the most technically advanced product does not in itself create market share.

UNIX has become the dominant standard mid-range operating system. Most of these mid-range systems have dumb character-based terminals connected and they offer a very cost-competitive solution to the computing requirements of small businesses and departments.

The client/server architecture described in this book assumes a graphical user interface. There are two UNIX solutions to this requirement: either X-terminals or UNIX workstations connected to a UNIX server, or OS/2 or Windows PCs connected to a UNIX server.

An X-terminal is a low-cost dumb terminal with a graphical user interface. The application runs on the main processor and the graphics run on the terminal. This can make a configuration of X-terminals connected to a UNIX machine appear much cheaper than a PC-based solution. The reality is that a small number of intensively used, graphical X-terminals will bring even the largest server to its knees with the result that the configuration will cost more than one based on PCs.

The other UNIX solution is for the client machine to be running Windows or OS/2, attached to a UNIX database server. The is a cost-effective solution that is widely used in the corporate environment.

The use of graphical workstations running UNIX, usually on RISC hardware, is mainly limited to engineering and trading system workstations. The expansion of the UNIX workstation market is limited by the resources they require when run on Intel machines, their inability to run DOS and Windows applications efficiently and the difficulty of using them.

On top of these problems, there is no binary standard supported by all the UNIX vendors who for years have been creating incompatible versions. The realization that their market could be destroyed by Windows NT has resulted in an agreement on standards. It remains to be seen how long it will take for these standards to be implemented and then become widespread enough to exist as a force in the market. Meanwhile, Microsoft will not be waiting for the UNIX vendors to get their act together. For these reasons, UNIX (in all of its varieties) is seen as the third force on the desktop.

The Apple Mac is widely used in many market areas, principally desktop publishing, graphics and sophisticated home users. As the Windows and OS/2 user interfaces become increasingly easy to use, it becomes harder to see the Mac System 7 as anything other than a special-purpose operating system designed for proprietary hardware. To address this, Apple is putting a lot of effort into building a new generation of operating system based on non-proprietary hardware – the IBM PowerPC manufactured by IBM and Motorola. The success of this evolution remains to be seen. The Mac has many loyal users and the objective of Apple must be to keep their support while moving to a less proprietary and more open architecture. The uncertainty behind this, and Apple's current lack of market share in the client/server market, have put them in fourth place.

UNIX and open standards

The benefits of UNIX as a standard have been much exaggerated, but it has nevertheless become a widely used operating system, especially for mid-range computers.

UNIX is an attempt at an open industry standard that would prevent users from becoming locked into a particular hardware manufacturer. Unfortunately, in practice the UNIX standard does not deliver on this promise in the same way as the PC standard.

There are many types of standard. The strongest is typified by the PC, where an application written for one PC will run unchanged on any other PC. This binary compatibility has created the PC shrink-wrap software product market.

The UNIX standard is much weaker than this. There are varieties of UNIX standards for programming interfaces, binary compatibility and graphical user interfaces. With careful planning and choice of UNIX standards, applications can be ported between machines and operating environments in the same family.

There are two UNIX camps – Open System Foundation (OSF) and UNIX International. IBM is one of the members of OSF and Sun is one of the members of UNIX International. Many companies belong to both camps. There is also a 'United Nations' called X/Open which is trying to set a single standard and bring the two camps together.

The standard graphical user interface for OSF is Motif and the standard for UNIX International was Open Look. The COSE consortium has now agreed that Motif will become the single UNIX user interface standard.

The UNIX market is divided between two architectures. One consists of dumb terminals attached to a central minicomputer running the application, the other applications with a graphical user interface. A graphical user interface requires either X-terminals or a network of graphical workstations. What is needed by many organizations is a standard graphical user interface, a binary standard that supports DOS and Windows applications, and UNIX connectivity. This is a description of both Windows and OS/2.

This configuration, of a UNIX server and Windows or OS/2 clients, plays to the strength of each and is supported by many computer manufacturers. Both Windows and OS/2 efficiently support DOS and Windows applications and provide a much easier environment to use than UNIX. They are therefore ideal for the client machine.

A very important standard in both the UNIX and the IBM world is the Open Software Foundation (OSF) Distributed Computing Environment (DCE). This provides transparent distributed computing across heterogeneous platforms. DCE is becoming the *de facto* standard for distributed computing in a multi-vendor environment and it is a key part of IBM's distributed systems strategy. IBM already provides DCE for AIX/6000 and intends to support it on MVS/ESA, VM/ESA, OS/2, OS/400 and AIX/ESA. It has also been agreed as a standard in Japan, by the European Commission and as part of X/Open.

DCE includes a wide range of services for managing global network computing, including remote procedure calls (RPC), a distributed file system, single logon to access global resources, and user and data security. RPC allows a programmer to use a procedure without knowing where the server providing that procedure resides. It enables calls to flow across an open network, handling authentication, authorization, encryption, time synchronization and automatic data format conversion.

Hardware

The two hardware architectures fighting for control of the desktop are those based on Intel and those based on RISC (Reduced Instruction Set Computing).

The Intel chip is associated with the success of the PC. The first PC had a 16-bit Intel chip with an 8-bit data path known as the 8088. This was followed at intervals of approximately two to three years by the 8086, 80286, 80386 and 80486. The most recent Intel chip is called the Pentium and the next two chips are already on the drawing board. Intel has demonstrated a consistent and smooth fall in price/performance over the years and this shows no sign of abating.

A few years ago pundits proclaimed the end of the Intel chip. They maintained that its architecture was inherently and fundamentally limited and that within a few years it would be replaced by a new generation of chips based on RISC. In fact, some of those industry pundits speculated that Microsoft put so much effort into producing a RISC version of Windows because they were worried that they would become stuck with the Intel chip as it became yesterday's technology.

The Intel chip is still with us, and there are two reasons why. The first is that the Intel architecture had and still has more life in it than forecast. This is partly because Intel is currently selling 10 million 486 chips a year and so can fund a massive research program. This gives Intel many technical options. For example, it could develop the '686' chip as a RISC processor with the Intel instruction set hard-wired into it. It appears that not only is Intel planning this but so also are RISC manufacturers. It also appears that IBM is considering hard-wiring the Intel instruction set into its PowerPC, so the eventual result may be that it is not a choice between RISC or Intel but RISC plus Intel from everyone.

The second reason is simply that for a PC user to switch to a workstation based on a RISC chip, the price/performance when running existing DOS and Windows binaries must be greater than a workstation based on an Intel chip. Should this happen, the change to RISC would take place rapidly. On a RISC machine, NT runs existing Intel binaries slowly (as it uses software emulation). However, software vendors who recompile their products can provide higher levels of price/performance than those on an Intel chip. The question remains whether users will be willing to replace all their existing software.

The interesting players to watch in the RISC market are DEC and IBM. DEC has staked their future on the Alpha chip. Although this is a powerful and low-cost chip, it will be difficult for DEC to succeed in selling the Alpha in PC volumes. Nevertheless, DEC will achieve a substantial early market for its Alpha chip because of its existing customer base and its ability to run VMS applications. As DEC is committed to the long haul, it will inevitably become a major force in the RISC market.

IBM, Apple and Motorola announced their joint development of the PowerPC chip in October 1992. This RISC chip is based on the design of the RISC System/6000. This is a very advanced design that was difficult to implement on a single chip. However, the consortium succeeded and the result was the next generation of Apple Mac machines. More significantly, IBM will be launching its own family of products based on the PowerPC. These will run AIX, Windows NT and the Workplace OS operating systems.

Summary

This chapter has looked at the desktop machine, the operating system and the type of processor needed for client/server applications.

The conclusion is that client/server development requires 32-bit performance, multi-tasking, the ability to efficiently run DOS/Windows personal productivity applications, and good, stable communications and database support. The only operating systems that currently provide these are OS/2 and Windows NT.

Two important new products should arrive in 1995 – Windows 95 from Microsoft and Workplace OS from IBM. Windows 95 will be an upgrade from Windows 3.1 that tens of millions of users are likely to take. Workplace OS will enable IBM to provide a version of OS/2 that runs on their new Power PC machines.

The processor is likely to remain Intel-based at least until 1997, but RISC machines, especially the DEC Alpha and those based on the IBM PowerPC, will play an increasingly important role.

CHAPTER 4

DEVELOPMENT TOOLS

In the early 1950s, when there were only six computers in the world, the shortage of programmers was the bottleneck that held back their exploitation. Today, when the number of computers exceeds 100 million, it is still the bottleneck. How can programming be made easier? Or is this the wrong question? Should it be: Why program at all?

Programming languages were the first step up the ladder of finding increasingly productive ways of building applications. Conventionally, programming means learning a language with an obscure syntax (the rules for putting things together) and even more obscure semantics (what things mean). This has taken skilled people months or years to learn and still applications contain many mistakes.

The next step up the ladder was tools to assist with parts of the development process. These tools included screen painters and code generators for file maintenance applications. Unfortunately, it was found that although they speeded up the development of simple demonstration applications, they offered little benefit for typical commercial applications.

These tools were followed by sophisticated mainframe 4GLs that were suitable for large application development and offered real productivity improvements. On the PC, simpler applications were required and a new class of database language product became popular, typified by dBASE.

Three technology trends overtook these two types of development tool – the GUI, the SQL database and high-end client/server (that is, the use of PCs to implement applications that formerly would have been implemented on the mainframe).

What is needed is a new type of 4GL which exploits the GUI, supports SQL databases and runs on the PC but provides features formerly only found in mainframe 4GLs. A detailed list of requirements for such a 4GL is given in Table 4.1.

Meanwhile, users have learned to use increasingly sophisticated tools, such as spreadsheets and databases, and have built simple applications for themselves. This has blurred the distinction between programming and using tools to get a job done. Spreadsheets make it easy to build simple applications because they are visual.

Think again about screen painting. Painting a screen is not like programming in a conventional language – it is easy to learn and mistakes are obvious because they can be seen immediately. But it is an alternative, so how can conventional programming languages be made this visual? Can the logic of a program be painted in the same way as a screen?

Lastly, this chapter discusses object-oriented programming. The term 'object-oriented' and the abbreviation 'OO' are found everywhere as a panacea. Objects seem to be discussed in almost every article written about software development, but if we look at object-oriented languages we find the technology does not, in itself, address the basic requirements. There are some concepts that, if correctly implemented within a set of tools, can simplify some programming problems. However if the basic requirements are ignored then the result can be worse than before. Most object-oriented programming languages still have a very complex syntax and semantics.

The key mistake is thinking that by making programming languages more complex they will become better tools for everyone and for all applications. Tools must be designed with their use and their user in mind. For large commercial applications the tools must suit commercial programmers and the requirements of large-scale commercial development.

Complex languages always mean long training times and programs that are difficult to maintain. To compound the problem, programming languages are usually 'sensitive' rather than 'robust'. A sensitive language is one in which a change to a single character can result in a syntactically valid statement with a completely different meaning. A robust language is one in which a large, visible change is required to give a large change in meaning.

The challenge is to create a robust language with simple syntax and semantics which can be used to develop large applications and which provides all the benefits of object-oriented programming.

Requirements for development tools

A development tool is a software system for producing and maintaining applications. The requirements listed in Table 4.1 are for the features needed in development tools used to produce high-end client/server applications with a GUI.

Table 4.1 Development tool requirements.

1. High-end	Is it 32-bit and does it fully support multi-tasking?
2. Team development	Does it support dictionary-based development, modular programming and version control?
3. Productivity	Is it easy to learn? Is it a 'robust' language? Will it still be productive when the application is large?
4. Maintenance	Is there a language with simple syntax and semantics, and is there good impact analysis support?
5. Database support	Does it support a wide range of SQL databases and stored procedures/static SQL?
6. Prototype	Does it support the full GUI with user involvement in window painting and business logic?
7. Platform independence	Does it produce applications that run on the major client operating systems?
8. General integration	Does it have good integration to other applications running locally?
9. Communications	Does it support a wide range of communications methods to applications running remotely?
10. Program delivery	Is there an effective delivery mechanism for the finished application?
11. Object-oriented	Does it support the OO user interface and all the necessary programming constructs?
12. Support	Is there good hot-line support and training and consultancy services available?
13. Strategy	Does the supplier have a well-thought-out strategy for product enhancement?
14. Track record	Are there reference customers?

Types of development tool

There are many types of development tool (shown in Table 4.2). The categories overlap but the list forms a useful starting point. Each category is discussed in more detail later to show how they more or less meet the above requirements.

Programming languages

Writing client/server applications is difficult, expensive and risky, yet many organizations are switching from mainframe COBOL development to C or C++ programming for the workstation. Of all the possible mistakes, this is potentially the most serious. After years of mainframe development, MIS departments have dug themselves into a maintenance hole. It is estimated that about 80% of development expenditure is for software maintenance. This would be fine if all the required systems were in place and the maintenance work was keeping them up-to-date. Unfortunately, this is not the case. Users are crying out for new systems to keep the organizations competitive and MIS departments cannot respond.

In these circumstances it might be thought that the last thing to occur is for those organizations to start new client/server applications using a language that is inherently harder to learn and more costly to maintain than COBOL, namely C/C++. (Although C++ has benefits over C for systems programming, the arguments regarding their suitability for commercial development apply equally to both. To signify this they are referred to jointly as C/C++.) However, this is precisely what is happening in many organizations. The reasons are that C/C++ has been marketed as the COBOL of the future. In 1993 the number of advertised jobs for C/C++ programmers exceeded those for COBOL program-mers for the first time. It is true that C/C++ is the best language for writing operating systems, personal productivity tools, compilers, device drivers and

Table 4.2 Types of development tool.

1. Programming languages

2. Code generators

3. Database and GUI front-ends

4. CASE tools

5. 4GLs

utilities, and it is also true that there is a vast new industry employing C/C++ programmers to write these things, but this does not mean that C/C++ is the best language in which to write commercial client/server applications.

The backlash will come over the next three years as organizations find their original C/C++ programmers have moved on and the applications they leave behind must be maintained. Have you ever tried recruiting a C/C++ programmer to maintain complex GUI client/server code?

C/C++ programming

C/C++ is a low-level programming language that provides complete control over the way the operating system is used. It is ideal for writing tools, utilities and system software. However, there are a number of dangers with the use of C/C++ for commercial development:

- The C/C++ programming environment for building graphical client/server applications is extremely complex. There are, for example, approximately 2000 calls to learn, just to handle the user interface. This means that C/C++ programmers are in short supply and are an expensive resource.

- The C/C++ programming language itself is very sensitive, that is, a small change to a single statement can result in the program working completely differently. Another way of putting this is to say that serious mistakes are easy to make and are not prevented by the language.

- It is unusual to find a good C/C++ programmer who is also a business analyst. C/C++ programmers are motivated to produce technically sophisticated solutions. Commercial applications should be built with the user, and business analysis skills are vital.

- C/C++ programmers find the graphical user interface challenging and exciting to write for today, but when the excitement has passed who will maintain the applications? It is notoriously difficult to maintain a C/C++ program written by someone else.

- The C/C++ programmer is often motivated to get the best from the technology – 'because it's there'. Unfortunately, this is not necessarily what the end-user needs.

- Enforcing standards, such as user interface design guidelines, requires external control as C/C++ itself enables any type of user interface to be built.

- Prototyping is difficult and laborious because of the time required to develop and modify C/C++ programs, and because the programs themselves cannot be understood by the end-user.

Having said all that, C/C++ programming skills can be very valuable on a project when correctly applied. If a specialist device driver is required, such as a non-standard communications link or a special interface, then C/C++ is the language to use.

In short, use C/C++ programmers only where and when you would use them on a conventional mainframe project.

Code generators

A code generator is a high-level development tool that generates the application as 3GL program code, such as COBOL, C, C++ or BASIC. Typically, these products assist with little more than the GUI screen generation and all of the application logic needs to be coded directly in the 3GL. They are therefore productive in the GUI development stage, but productivity drops off rapidly (usually to the level of the chosen language) as soon as you move on to the rest of the application.

Code generators were first developed because programmers realized that they were writing the same, or similar, code over and over again. This was particularly true for tasks such as the file maintenance operations on a data record (create, retrieve, update, delete and print). However, the logic of an application needs to be expressed in a language and it is here that code generators fail to deliver. The application logic must be written in the third-generation programming language. This means productivity also suffers because linking the GUI code to the application logic is an extra stage in development. In some cases, it is difficult to reuse the code generator after the programmer has added the application logic.

If the application is going to be developed in a 3GL, then a code generator can be a fast way of creating the initial screens and getting the project underway, but once underway the majority of the application will be written in the 3GL.

Code generators appear to offer the best of two worlds – standard languages and high-level application creation. Instead they typically offer the worst of both worlds – low-level programming and limited high-level creation.

GUI and database front-ends

These tools are designed to enable simple GUI applications to be developed rapidly. They are aimed at single developers and have limited database, communications and team development facilities. They range from simple window painters, such as the Dialog Editor, which are designed to be used with other languages, through to languages such as Visual BASIC and Power-Builder, which are designed to produce complete applications.

Database front-ends are typically sold by the database vendors as a simple way of building applications in front of their database. The classic example of this type of product is dBASE. This is a language and a database combined and is suitable for building simple departmental database-oriented applications. More recent examples range from Microsoft's Access and Borland's Paradox through to the front-end tools supplied by Oracle and Ingres.

Front-end development tools are at one end of the 4GL spectrum so they can be seen as a limited type of 4GL. How far they are along the spectrum depends on how the particular front-end tool matches up to the requirements described below in the section on 4GLs.

They offer very good database integration to the particular database they are designed around but generally they are poor at accessing other databases and general communications tasks.

CASE tools

Computer Assisted Software Engineering (or CASE) is one of those technologies that became fashionable, was oversold by the vendors, grew to a substantial market and is now in decline. The decline is not because of a fundamental problem with the approach but rather that the particular tools became unsuitable for the job. They became so large and complex that customers had to bet their organization, or at least their IT department, on the tool.

Also the tool vendors stayed for too long with an approach that was becoming dated. Their products focused on mainframe development to the exclusion of the workstation and the requirements of client/server. They had no or very poor support for graphical user interfaces, and their products were based on a 'waterfall' model of development that is being replaced by iterative development using newer 4GLs – also called Rapid Application Development (RAD) tools.

The waterfall model is based on stages. Each stage needs to be completed before the next can proceed, similar to water descending a waterfall. The waterfall model is associated with massive, detailed specifications which the user is asked to sign in blood! The development team then usually goes away for months or even years until eventually the final system is unveiled, often to the complete dismay of the user, who has not visualized the implications of the specification in terms of the usability of the final system.

The alternative is iterative development. This also encourages developing the application in stages, but each stage is a complete mini-project with its own specification, design, programming, testing and delivery. A mini-project might only be a few weeks long and is unlikely to be more than a few months. During development, the user participates in the process and is involved in the design and programming. The advantage is that quality, both in terms of fewer bugs and conformance with user requirements, is an inherent part of the process. Also, a finished product is delivered on a regular basis, allowing overruns and slippage to be more apparent and action to be taken as the project proceeds. As functionality is added incrementally, it automatically implements the KISS ('Keep It Simple, Stupid') principle.

The iterative development process requires different types of tool. The tools need to be more flexible and they need to include the programming phase as part of the process rather than as something that goes on in a back room. The tools usually center around a 4GL supported by data modeling, reverse engineering, project management and version control capabilities.

By using a 4GL, a business analyst sitting with the user can be creating the application as it is being specified. Use of such a 4GL in conjunction with conventional CASE tools would take place after the definition of the logical process and data structures.

A full life-cycle CASE tool would be used to define:

- The data flow diagrams (the business flows, showing external entities, such as *Customer* linked to processes, such as *Process sales*, which in turn are connected to data stores, such as *Products*).

- The entities (things important to the business about which data needs to be stored, such as *Customers*, *Suppliers* and *Products*).

- The entity relationships (the one-to-one, one-to-many and many-to-one relationships between entities).

- The logical processes.

The entities and entity relationships would eventually be transformed into the physical SQL database and from there into the 4GL.

The process specification would be the starting point for creating the 4GL's application logic. The designer would use the 4GL to create a good user interface, adding menus, pop-up windows, list boxes, buttons and so on.

However, this is a CASE-centric view of development that still regards the 4GL as just another type of programming language. A better model for development and for the role of various tools is 4GL-centric.

Fourth-Generation Languages (4GLs)

There are a wide range of development tools described as 4GLs. The typical features one would expect are shown in Table 4.3.

As explained in Chapter 3, any operating system suitable for the development of client/server applications must be 32-bit, support multi-tasking, provide extensive database facilities and have a full range of connectivity options.

The use of 4GLs for client/server development places them at the center of a set of application support tools. This 4GL-centric view of development moves the use of CASE tools, such as those for data modeling, to the periphery.

Table 4.3 Requirements of a 4GL.

1. Easy to learn

2. Suitable for developing a wide range of business applications

3. High-productivity graphical development environment

4. Produces structured programs that are easy to maintain

5. Includes a complete high-level programming language

6. Includes a graphical window painter

7. Provides comprehensive database and communications support

8. Supports team development

9. Preferably should provide support for object-oriented programming to a greater or lesser extent

10. Provides a sophisticated run-time architecture for managing memory, module loading, graphical controls, database and communications

Another critical area is the use of impact analysis tools. These make it easy to maintain, modify and reuse the application. A good impact analysis tool will extract all the entity and entity relationships from the completed application. The lack of this information lies at the heart of the problem of maintaining applications programmed using some 4GLs.

Many 4GLs still have an underlying language in which it is difficult to remember what to type (complex syntactically) and then, later, what it does (complex semantically). Look for a language that is easy to learn and produces programs that are easy to maintain.

When a large application has been completed in a conventional language, it becomes impossible to see where variables are used, modified, displayed and tested, whether their validation and format are consistent across modules and where a procedure defined in one module is used across the complete system.

Without this information, applications developed using this type of 4GL become difficult to maintain. A good impact analysis tool combined with a 4GL can overcome these problems and offer the benefits normally only provided by upper-CASE tools, along with the flexibility and ease of use of the 4GL (see Figure 4.1).

It seems from the above analysis that a 4GL is the best development tool to use to implement a high-end client/server application. But which 4GL? To answer this question each of the requirements is considered and explained in detail below.

Chapter 5 includes a weighted checklist that can be used to score and rate 4GLs.

1. High-end features

The 4GL must fully support the development of 32-bit multi-tasking applications. 32-bit support is required for performance and to exploit the full linear addressing range offered by 32-bit operating systems. This addressing range enables large tables to be handled in memory for efficient access and processing.

The requirement for multi-tasking is a requirement for a 'non-stop' user interface. If the user initiates a 30-second mainframe access then the user should be able to continue interacting with the application while the data access proceeds in the background.

True multi-tasking support brings with it a host of related requirements. Because parts of the application may be running asynchronously, there needs to be a way for tasks to communicate and 'handshake' over access to shared data. There also needs to be a way to start and stop tasks, some form of 'instance data' for each task, an inter-task communication method and the synchronization of task by means of semaphores.

2. Team development

Corporate client/server projects typically involve four to six programmers, but can involve many more. To support effective development, programmers must be able to work on their own modules, yet be able to integrate these into the total system easily.

A version control system is needed to control access to modules to prevent two developers working on the same module at the same time, yet to enable many developers to be using the same module simultaneously. A version control system also maintains a history of changes so that modules can, if necessary, be returned to a previous known state.

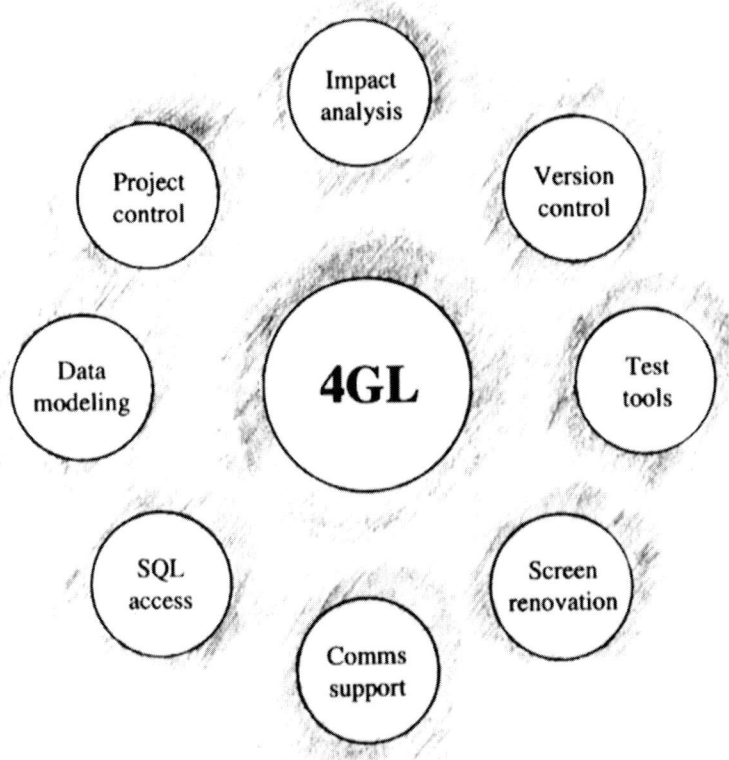

Figure 4.1 4GL development tools.

Each module developed must have its own local data and procedures and a well-defined external interface. The modules and their external interface should be recognized by the development environment so that dictionaries are updated automatically with the new functionality.

When the application is running it must be possible to load modules either on demand or when the application starts. One problem often encountered is that loading a single module cascades through the system and results in every module being loaded automatically.

3. Productivity and ease of use

Over the last 40 years, literally thousands of programming languages have been created. These languages have focused on features rather than usability. This has resulted in vast edifices such as the Ada language. Such languages contain all the features anyone could dream of but it takes months of intensive training before users can start to apply them. As a result, many organizations stay with COBOL, which was first defined in 1954.

A different approach is possible. By using the graphical environment to the fullest and combining the editor and the compiler, the programming syntax that needs to be learned can be kept to a minimum.

The graphical environment can also be used to represent the logic of the application directly. Instead of a syntactically complex language with obscure semantics, the developer can paint the logic of the application as easily as windows are painted in a screen painter. When combined with other features, such as pop-up dictionaries, graphical logic displays and outliners, such systems offers rapid, simplified entry of complex logic.

To determine the productivity increase attainable with a good 4GL, a major user in the US measured productivity with 'function point analysis', to determine how many functions were programmed in a man-month. The average mainframe project had previously been measured at 6.5, the best recorded was 18. The 4GL project recorded over 50 including the time needed to get programmers up to speed on the workstation, training on the 4GL and the normal problems associated with first-time usage.

Many 4GLs allow the program being developed to be run directly from the development environment without compilation and binding delay. The application can be run in 'trace' mode so that every procedure is animated and can be executed a line at a time or a complete procedure at a time.

When developing graphical user interfaces with such tools, rapid prototyping and short test cycles are made easy, and are essential for dealing with the wide variety of 'look and feel' options available to the programmer.

4. Maintenance

Low-cost software maintenance depends on understanding what has been developed and even more importantly being able to reuse programs that have been developed previously.

The key issue is whether someone, other than the developer, can come to the program months, or years, after it was developed, and understand what it does and all the implications of change.

If all the information exists in an upper-CASE tool and this corresponds exactly to the final delivered application, then the upper-CASE repository can be used to assess the impact of change. However, complex applications generated from an upper-CASE tool repository usually need to be modified by hand to create the final application. Once the application has been modified in this way the upper-CASE tool is no longer useful for maintaining it.

An alternative approach is to reverse-engineer the 4GL application that has been developed into an upper-CASE repository. Reverse engineering is the process of analysing a program listing in order to extract the structure of the logic of the application and the relationship between program and data. In this way all program changes are captured and the information is available for maintenance.

5. Database programming

SQL is a high-level language that defines data structures and manipulates data. Before SQL statements can be executed, they must be compiled into low-level instructions that are close to the physical structure of the database. Many SQL databases hide this compilation but IBM relational databases distinguish between two types of SQL – dynamic SQL and static SQL (see Chapter 2). Other types of SQL database enable pre-compiled SQL statements to be kept as stored procedures.

Static SQL and stored procedures are supported by C and by a few 4GLs. For maintenance purposes SQL statements should be kept together, ideally outside the program. If the database changes then searching hundreds of program modules for SQL statements is very time-consuming.

The use of static SQL becomes critical when the database is an IBM mainframe database, accessed and updated directly from a PC.

6. Prototyping and the GUI

Prototyping used to mean developing a simple application in COBOL or a 4GL to show the user what the screens would eventually look like. The prototype was then thrown away and the real application started.

Prototyping now refers to a development methodology perhaps better described as iterative application development. This consists of using a 4GL to develop small key parts of the total application. These parts are complete mini-applications which manipulate real data and which are put into production use. The application is then expanded from this base. Nothing is thrown away, although in the process of development parts may be rewritten.

A development methodology like this obviously calls for the close involvement of the end-user. There is no major specification sign-off stage and the techniques used to control and manage such projects are obviously very different from the conventional 'waterfall' approach.

The application development tool must enable the users to be involved in, understand and participate in the development process, and enable the developer to build to high standards without compromising quality.

An important point is that the more iterative the development process, the more important good project management becomes. Without a clear methodology, iterative development can degenerate into program hacking with no scope, control or timescales.

Within the constraints of a good development methodology, the checkpoints and controls assist the project manager in reducing the risk. Some aspects of project management are described in more detail in Chapter 5.

Another consideration for prototyping is that in order to produce the best user interface, the 4GL must be able fully to exploit the GUI of the operating system under which the application will run. Some 4GLs define their own GUI in order to make cross-platform support easier.

7. Platform independence

Another aspect of the 4GL is that it can insulate the organization from both the operating system and hardware decisions. A multi-platform 4GL enables the same application to be run under different operating systems and across different hardware platforms. An increasingly important aspect of corporate strategy must be to try to insulate each decision from the others so that if one aspect of the system changes (for example, a switch from Intel to RISC machines) the change does not ripple through the entire software system.

Although platform independence is important, the compromises made should be carefully considered. The minimum functionality that should be accepted for corporate client/server development is 32-bit, multi-tasking support with good communications and database support, and the ability to run DOS/Windows application efficiently. This means that the only currently acceptable and available platforms are OS/2 and Windows NT (see Chapter 3).

8. General integration

Users want to use applications that work together seamlessly. To achieve this the developer needs various types of 'glue'. This glue takes the form of communication methods and interfaces.

Software products typically provide a wide range of interfaces to other products: database, ASCII files, global dictionaries, memory sharing, function calling and command line parameters being a few. This results from the need to take into account the physical reality of the computer for performance reasons, and from a wide range of historical precedence.

As there must be interfaces to a wide range of products and systems, the design of which is outside the developer's control, the development tool must provide a wide range of interfaces.

Interfacing must also permit the use of products and applications together so that the facilities of one can enhance those of the other. If this can be done quickly, cleanly and transparently, each application will be seen as extending the functionality of the others.

There are therefore three integration requirements for a development tool:

- It must have a wide range of interfaces to enable it to interact easily with other software products or systems.

- It must provide a transparent interface between two parts of an application developed using the same tool.

- It must have a simple interface to other languages, such as C.

Many applications can be running at the same time on the same processor. The first requirement, therefore, is to be able to communicate between them effectively. Typically, a 4GL has three methods of intra-processor, inter-process communication: shared data, messaging and dynamic data exchange (DDE).

The ability to share memory dynamically between program modules provides a fast and transparent way for applications to communicate.

The messaging system allows one application to be performing a task, such as reading a database, while the other is processing the data. The interface provides semaphore handling for interlocking tasks that require the same resource.

The third method for allowing two applications to communicate is use of the DDE communications protocol. This is supported by a wide range of products, including spreadsheets and word processors. The DDE interface could be used, for example, to send data from a database application to a business graphics package to chart the data.

Finally, there are many specialist integration requirements that are project specific. For example, one project may want to integrate to a set of pre-defined routines, written in the C programming language, for mathematical analysis. Another project may require an image to be retrieved and displayed.

These 'one-off' requirements are typically programmed in C, and as a result the 4GL needs an easy way to link to such functions.

9. Communications programming

Have you ever tried to get a communications program working? If you have, then you know that communications programming can be extremely difficult. Why is this? It is a combination of programming problems – having to program at a low-level, handling real-time events, being in the correct communications state at the right time and defining communications buffers.

Typically, high-level programming languages are as bad as low-level languages. The only support they provide is through low-level functions. What is required is a way of dealing with communications at a transaction level, to have communication state change automatically handled by the system and to have all communication definitions, including buffers and data types, defined outside the program code.

10. Program delivery

Line-of-business client/server applications can involve application code running on hundreds or even thousands of workstations. It is important to consider the logistics of upgrading these systems when new versions of the application are released.

The first point is that the code should only reside on the file server. From here it is loaded dynamically across the LAN to the client workstation. This reduces the logistics problem to one of upgrading all file servers.

The finished application should be a self-contained set of files that can be easily distributed on diskette or across a network. The development system should never need to be distributed. More important, it should be easy to distribute a new release without sending the complete application. If the distribution is by diskette, then a new release might be a single diskette compared with ten for the complete application, with corresponding saving in installation time.

If distribution is by down-loading from a mainframe to servers, then the savings come in the transmission time and reduced costs. This becomes very important for an organization with more than a few hundred sites – say bank branches or retail shops.

A development tool should be used that enables the application to be developed as a set of separately loadable modules. To update the system, only the changed modules need to be down-loaded to the servers.

11. Object-oriented programming

Object-oriented programming holds the promise of low-cost maintenance and program reuse. It is one of those subjects that generates much debate about what is 'real' object-oriented programming but little discussion of practical commercial benefits. The debates are very similar to those that have taken place over the years about what is a real relational database, or what is a real expert system. Luckily, over time, the debates subside and the genuinely useful parts of the technology enter the mainstream.

The great benefit of object-oriented programming is the increased potential for reusable code. Corporations spend millions on developing software that, once completed, becomes difficult to change and is rarely reused on other projects.

In the past, similar benefits were claimed for modular programming. Modular programming emphasizes the benefits of subdividing the programming into independent modules. Each module can be independently developed and tested, and conventionally such modules will be combined at a link stage to create the finished executable program. The link stage resolves external references from one module to another. With large systems, the linked program can become monolithic and it can become increasingly difficult to modify a module and enhance the system.

Before showing how object-oriented programming solves this problem, some of the new terminology needs to be explained. It is easiest to explain using an example. Imagine you are designing an order entry system. The objects you will need are things like customers and order forms. Each particular customer and each completed order form is an *object*. Obviously all customers have a lot in common – there is a *class* called customer. Particular customers, such as 'Mr. Jones' are *instances* of that class ('instance of a class' is just another term for object). An object, such as 'Mr. Jones', consists of values linked to the object (such as his age and address) and chunks of program code. The chunks of program code are called *methods* and are associated with the class. A method is executed in response to a *request* and a *message* is used to carry the request and any results. A request is like a procedure call with zero, one or more parameters.

The data associated with an object cannot be altered except by executing a method (which is similar to calling a procedure). This hiding away of data is called *encapsulation*.

When a request is made, the particular method that is used depends on the target object (the one the request is sent to). This is called *polymorphism*. For example, if a print request is sent to a customer object then a customer record will be printed, if it is sent to an order form object then an order form will be printed. Another way of looking at this is to say that different classes can have methods with the same name, whereas in conventional programming languages all procedures must have unique names.

Finally, classes can be linked together in a *class hierarchy*. For example, an order form, purchase order and an invoice are all types of forms. A method can be defined for the general class, for example, the form class could have a print method that will print any type of form. Then if the order form does not have a print method, the general form print method will automatically be used instead. This is called *inheritance*.

The key benefits that can be realized from all this new terminology are that applications can be easier to maintain and code can be easier to reuse.

However, these benefits are not always, or even easily obtained. The debate raging at the moment is how to write systems so that code can be reused. A common recommendation is that once a class hierarchy has been implemented it should not be changed. If it needs to be modified later then it should be copied, renamed and the new version modified. This is because inheritance can cause a small change made to a general class to unexpectedly effect many other classes throughout the system.

This is horrific. We are switching to object-oriented programming to reduce maintenance costs and we find that it becomes impossible to maintain parts of the system. Even COBOL was not that bad. However, this does not mean we should throw it all away and go back to COBOL programming, but rather that we must proceed with care, expect no magic solutions and learn from our mistakes.

It is true that the interface between objects is clean. An object can therefore be removed and replaced by a different object, and so long as it handles the same messages the rest of the system cannot tell the difference. This means that, in theory, systems can be maintained locally (that is, by changing a single object without needing to understand the complete system). Of course, this is also true of any system that allows modules to be dynamically linked at run-time.

The opposite approach is demonstrated by a large monolithic COBOL program. Because there is a single Data Division that is used by all the procedures, it is necessary to understand how all the procedures use the data before changing any line of the program. For example, if I change the use of flag TMP-FLAG-1 so that it now has three values, will this upset any other part of the program?

Let us examine what has been learned about object-oriented programming:

- Because object-oriented techniques involve new concepts, new terminology and new methodologies, their introduction requires a substantial investment by an organization and a period where mistakes will be made.

- Object-oriented programming typically requires a language with complex syntax and semantics. This makes the language difficult to learn and applications difficult to maintain.

- Sometimes object-oriented program code cannot be reused as easily as suggested. One reason has already been given – the use of a complex language – but the other arises from the dangers of inheritance. One approach to this is not to use inheritance and this can prove a very effective solution, especially for the development of commercial applications. A second reason is more fundamental and has nothing to do with object-oriented programming – it is just that it is impossible to design in flexibility for the unknown. If the task is to build a graphics library, then a flexible solution can be provided because the problem is static and clearly bounded. However if the task is to build a custom business system, then flexibility cannot be built in, as the requirement is organic and open-ended. As the business changes, objects previously defined are found to have their boundaries incorrectly defined. It is then not a matter of replacing one object with another, but of redesigning all the objects. This is not a problem that can be addressed by taking longer with the design – it is simply a basic engineering fact. The lesson to learn from this is expressed in the riddle 'if it takes two years to write a set of reusable routines that are never used, were they ever reusable?'

- Business tasks are often very procedural and rule based. Object-oriented programming languages are generally not suited to expressing business logic clearly. Their use results in the creation of methods in which the business rules get lost in the complexity of object interaction. As the application does not then reflect the structure of the business rules, it becomes very difficult to maintain the application as the business rules change. The solution here is to combine procedural or rule-based programming with object-oriented programming.

- Some object-oriented tools do not easily fit with other products and languages. Object-oriented tools sometimes define their own operating environment, so they do not integrate easily with relational databases and other languages and subsystems.

- Many object-oriented tools are designed for a single developer, not for team development, that is to say they do not allow modular development with the dynamic linking of separately developed modules.

- Many object-oriented tools require that a very large run-time environment be supplied with the finished application. This makes applications unwieldy and difficult to distribute and update.

Some of these problems concern correct use of the technology, some are simply limitations of today's products and operating systems.

IBM has set out to solve some of the operating system problems with SOM (System Object Model) and Microsoft with OLE (Object Linking and Embedding).

Today each programming language and tool creates its own little world of objects, and these cannot speak to each other. SOM and OLE take objects out of the language and move them into the operating system. Objects can then be created in any language, all objects are equal and an object written in one language can communicate with an object written in another language.

When the operating system recognizes objects instead of programs, then they can be written in any language, including procedural languages such as C.

SOM and OLE are simply the first steps taken to integrate object-oriented concepts into the operating system. Both Microsoft and IBM are working on making their operating systems more object-oriented over the next five years. This means that over time many of today's problems will disappear as the technology becomes embedded in the operating system.

Today many object-oriented programming tools are complex technical toys. Their use requires skilled staff and can result in precisely the problems they seek to avoid. Planning to learn some of today's products is a waste of time and resources. It is analogous to learning how to maintain the engine before driving a car. Technology for its own sake is best avoided. Look for those tools that directly address the business issues. They should be productivity, easy to learn, support team development and result in genuinely maintainable systems.

Component programming

This chapter has made it clear why high-end client/server applications should be developed using a 4GL with a programming language that is robust, easy to learn and which supports the maintenance of large applications. But how will such tools incorporate the benefits of objected-oriented programming? This requires a new approach to development that Microsoft describes as 'component programming' and it requires new facilities in the operating system.

Component programming is a method of building applications that consist of separate objects recognized by the operating system. The term 'component' is used to distinguish such objects from the wide range of other objects that might co-exist in the system. In business applications components tend to be large and have a 'flat' class structure and so make little use of inheritance. They are such things as 'Customer', 'Customer List', 'Order Form' and 'Invoice'.

Components may be written in any language – C, C++, Smalltalk or a 4GL – and components communicate using the OO facilities of the operating system.

As OO facilities in the major operating systems are currently limited, this inhibits what can be done today but the next two years will see substantial OO facilities added to OS/2 and Windows, so it is now time to start planning the design of future systems based on the capabilities these facilities provide.

Component programming is based on two beliefs:

- The language used to write a component should depend on the nature of the component and its developer. If you are writing business components then you should use a 4GL that is easy to learn, can represent business rules and procedures naturally and results in programs that are easy to maintain.

- Components need to be recognized and communicate at the operating system level. Operating systems up to now recognize and run programs. Programs have some of the features of objects (such as encapsulation) but operating systems do not provide facilities for registering their methods and passing messages between them. This is changing with subsystems like SOM and OLE 2.0, which provide some of these facilities.

Object-oriented programming systems, such as Smalltalk, provide a closed OO world but no message-level communication with other OO worlds, such as C++. Object-oriented tools need to stop being inward looking and look outward to the operating system (see Figure 4.2).

With this architecture it is clear that the features of an object-oriented system, such as encapsulation, polymorphism and inheritance, must be provided by the operating system. When we look at SOM and OLE 2.0 and their future direction, we see them providing these features and many others that provide additional benefits which arise once the operating system takes responsibility for communication:

• Components can reside anywhere and communicate transparently. Future versions of SOM and OLE promise to provide message passing systems that allow components to communicate across a wide area network. So a component running on one machine can use a method provided by a component on another machine, without first needing to know where it is run.

• Components communicate using an industry-standard protocol. The industry standard for handling requests between objects is CORBA (the Common Object Request Broker Architecture). IBM plans to support this on top of DCE, and so enable components to communicate across different hardware platforms and operating systems.

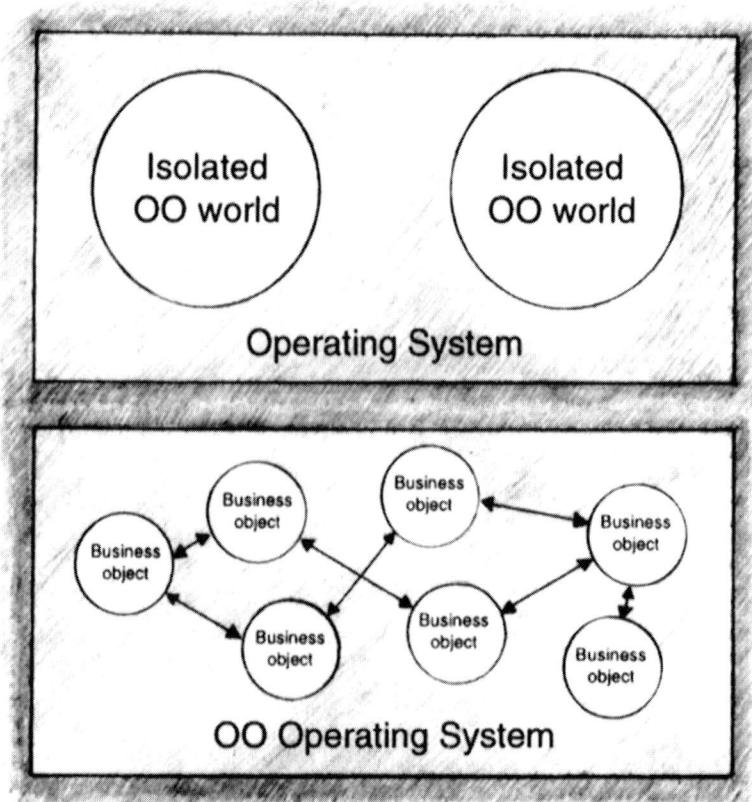

Figure 4.2 OO programming versus component programming.

- Components can be written in any language. Because of this the confusion between OO benefits and language benefits can be removed. With OO benefits provided by the OS we can look for a language that is suited for business application development and maintenance. OO languages, such as C++, can be used to write low-level graphics, database and communications facilities used by high-level business components.

- Components can be developed and sold by anyone and then used in any system being built. The language in which they were written is transparent. This means that we can look forward to a time when new systems are produced in the same way in which a garden is created rather than the way a house is built.

We have got used to thinking about development as a building process. This analogy is reinforced by terms such as 'software engineering', 'architecture' and 'design'. But there are, of course, alternatives to development, since application packages are bought, not built. The problem is that packages are inflexible and impossible or difficult to modify, even if written in a high-level language. The principle of buying a finished solution is correct but the problem is that application packages are written as monolithic systems, not as components.

If we think components then the analogy changes from building a system to growing a system. A garden is created by shopping for new things, swapping with friends and cloning what you have already. Any single component can be changed, moved or removed without changing any other component, but every change improves the overall effect.

It is true that each individual component must be built but this can often be done by assembling methods from other components that already exist. At the lowest level, programmers will still be building the basic components that others will be assembled from. The tools that are needed in future must, therefore, support the assembly of new components from existing components using the facilities embedded within the operating system.

This vision of the future of development is not short-term. Such changes typically take 10 to 15 years to come into widespread use. However, to be aware of how the development process is evolving helps with medium-term planning.

Summary

There is an enormous variety of tools available – all claim to be client/server, object-oriented, easy to use and highly productive. This chapter has tried to point out some of the benefits and some of the dangers and pitfalls in selecting development languages and tools.

The fundamental problem with most languages and development tools is that they have complex syntax and semantics and are sensitive to small changes. This makes them difficult to learn and makes programs difficult to maintain.

As with any commercial decision, the final choice of development tools is likely to be based more on credibility and track record rather than technology. In the end you choose the tool or language that seems most likely to be able to get the job done, within the timescales imposed.

CHAPTER 5

MANAGING THE PROJECT

Many of the guidelines given in this chapter are basically common sense and no different from the way that computer software has been developed for years. It does not try to tell you how to be a project manager, but instead assumes that you are one and that you are starting your first client/server application.

Developing software is inherently risky, but the biggest risk is that you choose to do nothing. This chapter is concerned with the best ways of managing that risk.

Selecting development tools

It is assumed that before you start the project you have chosen a suitable development tool. How do you choose between all the tools available? Table 5.1 gives a checklist of the points raised in the previous chapter.

To use the table, fill in the score as a number between 0 and 10 (0 is no such feature, 1 the lowest and 10 the highest), then multiply each individual score by the weight alongside it. Finally, add up the totals to give the overall score out of 1000.

Changing the business

It is important to realize before starting that client/server applications can change the way an organization does business. Take the example of sales order

Table 5.1 Selecting a development tool.

Requirement	Score	Weight	Total
1. High-end. Is it 32-bit and does it fully support multi-tasking?		10	
2. Team development. Does it support modular development?		10	
3. Productivity. Is it easy to learn? Will it still be productive when the application is large?		10	
4. Maintenance. Is there a language with simple syntax and semantics and is there a good impact analysis tool?		10	
5. Database support. Does it support a wide range of SQL databases and static SQL?		10	
6. Prototype. Does it support the full GUI with user involvement in painting and business logic?		5	
7. Platform independence		5	
8. General integration		5	
9. Communications		5	
10. Program delivery. Is there an effective delivery mechanism?		5	
11. Object-oriented. Does it support the OO user interface and programming constructs?		5	
12. Support. Is there good support, training and consultancy?		5	
13. Strategy. Does the supplier have a well-thought-out strategy for product enhancement?		5	
14. Track record. Are there reference customers?		10	
		Total	

entry. A typical mainframe order entry system would require the sales people to enter orders on an order form. This would then be keyed in by data entry clerks to create a file of orders that would be processed by the mainframe.

Think of the alternative. An application with a graphical user interface could be used directly by the sales people as a sales tool when sitting with the customer. Think how this technology can revolutionize the way any organization does business:

- A bank can turn its cashiers into sales people for all of its products and services, with automatic 'cross-selling'.

- A hardware manufacturer can supply the sales people with a system that advises on the best product and configuration, thus increasing revenue per sales person.

- A car rental company can provide a better service and optimize car usage.

- A car dealer sales person can use the system to work out the best financing option while sitting with the customer.

- A telesalesforce can be provided with more information to help it sell more effectively.

These types of applications cannot always be identified by looking at the current business. They arise from being aware of the potential of the technology and the overall business objectives (for example, to increase revenue per sales person). To become aware of the potential it is necessary to start by building some simple applications. This is why getting started is the most important step.

New methods for old

If you have spent years managing projects, especially fixed-price projects, then you will know that it is vital to produce a clear specification first. You must get the user to sign off on it and then manage changes like a hawk.

Unfortunately, graphical applications of the type we have been discussing cannot be developed in this way. It might be more accurate to say that although they might be developed in this way, the application will then not be getting the best from the graphical user interface.

As the graphical user interface usually involves a higher investment in hardware, it is important to gain maximum advantage from it. The way to do this is to prototype the application first. The prototype then becomes the specification and eventually the finished application. With a good 4GL, the prototype need not be thrown away and the application rewritten.

New standards are required to control this type of development. These include new standards for specification, documentation, design, user involvement and sign-off, programming, testing and delivery. If you are following a comprehensive conventional methodology, the changes needed can be very minor.

The current methods used for business analysis and modeling stay the same, although you must bear in mind that the technology offers new opportunities for the business.

The data modeling can be done using conventional tools and methods. This can be carried through to the creation of the physical database.

The logical process description can be fully analysed so long as this is done completely independently of the physical implementation. For example, a functional decomposition could become a menu structure with a conventional application. With an object-oriented user interface, it would not become a menu but the low-level logic would remain the same. The logic would be invoked by an event (such as dropping one object upon another) rather than from a menu.

The object-oriented design would result in a definition of the objects and their relationships. The objects correspond in many ways to the tables in the database, and the relationships are defined by the logic performed and the way in which they are invoked (by button, menu, direct manipulation and so on).

Many of the documentation standards remain the same. The new document needed is one to link actions with the response. The actions available are events such as button clicking, double clicking, selection and clicking, menu selection, direct manipulation and so on. Each action must be documented with the response it produces. The response would be documented as a conventional mini-spec or flowchart.

Art of the database

If you come from a mainframe background then you will find many of the mainframe database disciplines still apply. An application may be directly accessing and updating the mainframe database. The area in which you will need to build up skills and experience is building responsive, interactive PC applications with a graphical user interface.

If you come from a PC development background then you will find building a client/server application that uses an SQL database involves different considerations from using a PC database such as dBASE or Paradox. You will already have many of the skills needed to build a good user interface, but even here be careful, because building a graphical user interface requires new skills.

SQL appears to be a high-level language that makes it easy to write database applications, but it can be a wolf in sheep's clothing if approached in this way. The guidelines are:

- Carry out a proper database analysis. This ensures that the data is properly organized to avoid duplication, improve performance and simplify changes later.

- Identify the units of work, the 'locking' of data and the transaction interaction. For example, if the display shows one item of stock remaining, then by the time it has been ordered it may have already been taken by another transaction. In this case it will be necessary to recheck the value while updating it.

- If you are using a 4GL, then check that it supports static SQL and has facilities for tuning the SQL to optimize the performance of the finished application.

- Think about performance – a missing key or a key not used can change the response from a fraction of a second to minutes.

Project methodology

The biggest change is the move away from the old 'waterfall' model of development, where everything is agreed on in advance, to an interactive, iterative or prototyping approach. This approach can be thought of as a number of small projects each building upon the results of the previous one. Thinking about it in this way makes it clear that the old standards are not thrown away, but that they are being applied to each small project.

It can be argued that standards must be applied even more rigorously than in the past because each small project is built on the previous one – and for this to be successful each project must be correctly analysed, well designed and well documented.

Management methods

The overall management objectives are to focus on the business objectives, build an integrated development team, work in phases, and control and manage all changes.

One tricky question is that of project ownership. As business managers become more involved, define the benefits and sign up for delivery, there is a danger that no one is put in charge of the technical issues. It is vital that the IT project manager be fully accountable for delivering the finished application. However,

the business manager must own the actual achievement of the benefits. The IT
role is therefore a support role, not a leading role, in which the objective is to
provide high-quality results to the business units.

Business focus

The first thing is to make sure that everyone involved in the project understands
the business objectives and their benefits. The best way to achieve this is to
write them down. This may seem obvious but it is easily lost sight of in the
excitement of starting a new project (and not all projects are approved following
a careful analysis of the business benefits).

What needs to be covered is:

- What will the business be able to do that it could not do before?
- How much money does the business expect to save (if any)?
- How much new revenue does the business expect to gain?
- How will market share be increased?
- How will quality of service be improved?
- How will the success or otherwise of the project be measured? Will it be cost
  savings, market share increase, better quality or time saved?

Whatever the measure of success, start gathering information immediately.
This ensures that the information is actually being collected.

Targets should be set at the beginning of the project that are measurable,
realistic and related to the business objectives. These should then be agreed on
by everyone concerned as the measure of the success of the project.

This does not mean that you should focus on only the tangible benefits, as many
of the benefits of information technology are intangible. The primary question
should be 'is this a good business decision?' It is not a process of gathering
numbers to keep the accountants happy.

Intangible benefits can be measured, but this may involve subjective judgment
by senior line managers, market analysis or measuring related factors. For
example, being first to market can be measured by senior managers in terms of
lead time, building customer awareness by market analysis, and customer
satisfaction by the number of complaints received.

The IT project manager must gain commitment from the business. This is more
than just budget approval – a good indicator of commitment is the time the
business manager is willing to spend on regular project reviews.

The objective is for the business manager and IT manager to work closely together. When this happens, make sure it is clear what the responsibilities and authority of each are. Who 'owns' the project? Who will make the decisions?

Team building

Do not split the team into those who produce a specification and those who code it. Use people who can work at all levels. They must be capable of working with the users, they must have experience with designing a graphical user interface and they must be prepared to program modules.

One good indication of the right level of person is a programmer who wants to work at a much higher level than C. You also need to include on your team people who have genuine experience with the server interface. This might be, for example, SQL experience, CICS experience or APPC communications programming experience.

Phased delivery

The important thing is to start now. As mistakes are bound to be made (especially if this is your first client/server project), allow for this by spending the first month in building a *demonstrator*. A demonstrator tests the capabilities of the technology, enables you to evaluate the suitability of your chosen tools and results in a software program that you can use to get further 'buy-in' to the project. It also enables you to gather your first facts and make early decisions on estimating, testing, version control, distribution, standards and performance.

As it is called a demonstrator, expectations will be low and you will be able to throw it away if you want to change your approach. This does not mean you need to throw it away; it is often a good basis for continuing to the next stage, but it does give you that choice.

The next phase is the production of a *pilot system*. This is the first of the mini-projects that will eventually result in the complete application. The pilot system is up to four months long and results in a complete deliverable application. The application should do something useful, with a business benefit, and there should be no reason why it could not go into production use.

By the end of the pilot system phase, you must have written down, agreed to and put into effect the following:

- An estimating method that will be used for future stages. This will contain your own factors measured during development. Obviously these factors will be continually refined as further development is undertaken. There is no such thing as a finished estimating technique.

- A testing method, test tools and test plans should have been selected and put into use. Client/server applications with a graphical user interface are difficult into test thoroughly. This phase will therefore take more effort than you might have expended in the past. Testing should be done with a graphical test tool that can apply pre-prepared scripts. While this is essential for testing for regressions, a test tool does not avoid the need for human testing.

- A version control system should be in place to control the development process. It is essential that version control software be used and that no one can make changes outside this system. It is possible to develop your own version control system, but packages are available at low cost that do the job effectively.

- You should have worked out how the software will be distributed to users and how new versions will be incorporated at a later date. If you have twenty users connected to the same LAN, this is relatively straightforward. If you have five hundred users on fifty LANs in six countries, then ask IBM about SystemView or Microsoft about Systems Management Server (SMS).

- You should have finalized your programming standards and naming conventions, everyone should be following them and any code written prior to the standards being finalized should have been modified to bring it into line. It is more important that you have standards that everyone keeps to, than exactly what the standards are.

- Finally, you should have decided on the type of help system and produced the help system and user documentation for the pilot system. You should also have decided how these will be extended and how they will support the telephone hot-line support system you will also need.

The final phases of the project can now incrementally add functionality to the pilot system. You should aim to deliver new functionality at least every four months. For each stage, choose features that add business benefits.

This method of phased delivery has two fundamental benefits. The first is that it provides faster feedback from the users and the business. This will direct later stages and determine the new functionality to be added. Do not be afraid to change the user interface, but do not change it for change's sake.

The second benefit is that you have kept it simple. If there is one rule in software development that comes before all others, it is the one expressed by the acronym KISS – Keep It Simple, Stupid. Projects go wrong by trying to tackle too much, not by trying to tackle too little.

In the past, businesses have been so afraid that systems cannot be changed once delivered that they insisted on including all the bells and whistles. The result is that the project overruns, does not perform and never goes live. By developing in phases, you are allowing change and forcing the business to prioritize its requirements.

Estimating guidelines

You must produce your own estimating guidelines following the completion of the pilot phase. Table 5.2 gives you a rough starting point. Do not use the man-day estimates other than as guidelines, since they depend on the development tools you are using and the people you employ.

This is a high-level estimating technique. You can refine it by multiplying each estimate by a complexity factor (more for complex windows or complex SQL, less for simple ones) or you may want to go to function point analysis and measure all window fields, all window interaction events, all the logic points in your program and so on. Remember that productivity between different people can frequently be as much as 10:1!

Table 5.2 Estimating guidelines.

Activity	Man-days
Data model	3 days + 1 day per table
Database creation	2 days + 1 day per table
Database population	2 days + 1 day per table
GUI high-level design	5 days
GUI window design	1 day per window
Module architecture	5 days
Building GUI	1 day per window
Building SQL	2 days + 1 day per statement
Building communications	5 days + 1 day per transaction + server end
Building 3270/5250	5 days + 1 day per screen
Building utilities	1 day per public procedure
Building help	3 days + 1 day per window
Testing	1 day per window
Change requests	Add 20% to 50% to the estimate
Delivery	5 days + 1 day per 10 users

Controlling change

You must define procedures for managing all the changes that can take place. Each type of change will probably be documented on a different form which is signed by the relevant authority:

- Business changes that alter the primary objectives and overall requirement.

- Data model changes.

- Database changes.

- Design change requests, including user interface changes and enhancement requests.

- Error reports. These will come from the users as incident reports and be translated into error reports or design change requests by the project team.

- Program and module change requests, each usually corresponding to a design change or bug report.

It is important to determine how significant the change is to the person requesting it and to the business. The amount of work involved should be estimated and approval gained at the appropriate level before the extra work is scheduled.

Analysis methods

The analysis phase consists of producing a data model, creating a physical database and analysing the tasks. Data modeling software is recommended for this phase, but is not essential. If used, most products will create the physical database or generate the data definition language for creating the database.

The amount of time spent on this phase is difficult to estimate as it depends on the clarity of the business requirement. If the business requirement is clear and not likely to change, then a lot of time should be spent on creating the definitive data model for the complete project. The phases of the project can then concentrate on the user interface and connectivity issues. If the requirement is expressed at a high level and is not easy to translate into a data model, then spend a short time on this stage and allow time to modify it later. The demonstration phase is a good time to test the completeness and performance of the first data model.

Data modeling

Do the data modeling first (before you start programming) as it will clarify the whole analysis and design process.

Use conventional data modeling techniques:

- Entity descriptions
- Attribute type descriptions
- Entity–relationship diagrams (ERDs)

Produce a logical data model, as this will help you understand the system, and then follow up with the physical data model.

Think about balancing performance against the ease of maintaining the system. Most models go through a process of normalization, in order to understand the structure, and then de-normalization for performance reasons.

Database creation

If you are using an upper-CASE tool for data modeling (they are rarely used for anything else!) it should be used to create the database.

Populate the database with test data. If it exists elsewhere, then find a way to import it. Otherwise use the RDBMS to create one or two rows per table, export to a comma-delimited text file and then generate a realistic volume of data by copying records or by writing a special program.

You must be able to recreate the initial database test data for repeated testing.

Task analysis

This should only be done at the business level to document either current business practice or the new business requirement. Do not try to take this analysis to too low a level of detail. For example, you should not attempt to describe how the user will interact with the computer.

When describing a set of related actions it should not be assumed that one action must proceed another. If there is a business requirement to complete actions in a particular sequence then this should be documented, for example, by numbering the steps. This leaves the designer free to decide on the modality of the system.

With a graphical user interface, the user is in control of the sequence, and if a sequence of actions must be forced to occur in a particular order then this must be specifically programmed. This is unlike a conventional character-based system where the default behavior is a sequence of actions, and programming is necessary to escape in the middle and alter the sequence.

Design methods

The objective of design is to produce an application with a good user interface. This will involve working closely with the users and proceeding logically from the data model.

GUI guidelines

Designing a good user interface requires training, experience and a certain artistic flair. You should closely examine good user interfaces. Think about how they work, why they feel right and how menus, windows, controls, graphics and color are used.

There are a number of good books on GUI design including the IBM CUA Guide, the Microsoft style guide (*The Windows Interface: An Application Design Guide*, in the Windows SDK) and the Apple style guide (*Human Interface Guidelines: The Apple Desktop Interface*).

The aim of mainframe screen design is to pack all the necessary fields on each screen so that as much as possible can be displayed or entered with a single screen transfer. The aim of graphical screen design is to present the data clearly and to make all the actions obvious. The amount of data presented should be reduced dramatically and additional information can be made available by clicking a button. Far more information can be made available this way than with a conventional screen. For example, a combo box can display an option rather than requiring users to remember codes; it displays a button to list all the permitted options.

The user must be actively involved in the design of the windows and the interaction. It must be remembered that the use of the application may be dramatically different from conventional applications. For example, rather than pure data entry, users could enter data while sitting and talking to a customer. This means the dynamics of the customer interaction must be taken into account. For example, it may be better to enter financial information first, to get the customer to agree to the deal, before entering customer details such as name and address.

The goals are to increase the users' productivity and their satisfaction with the system, and to reduce their error rate. Design all of your windows in the same way and make the user interface consistent both within the application and with other products. You should produce an in-house style guide so that there is a consistency across all of your developments. In this way a user can transfer knowledge more easily between different applications.

Try to document the users' conceptual model. Talk to the users about how they see the system, especially any parts they find unclear.

Use color carefully; notice that good software products use color very discreetly and often a lot of gray.

Aim to make your windows modeless (that is, the user is not prevented from accessing a related window), but this does not need to be taken to extremes. A window that requires a user decision, such as an error window, can be made application-modal (a modal window is one that the user must interact with before continuing).

Design principles

The primary aim is to place the user in control so that there are no program-driven sequences. The appearance of the screen should 'speak for itself' so the user can see what needs to be done. If a number of actions need to be completed before the next stage can be started, you do not need to force the user to do them in order. Display ticks against the list of actions, allow the user to do them in any order and tick each as it is done. Check that everything is ticked before allowing the user to continue with the next stage.

Try to reduce the users' memory load by displaying all the information they require to make a decision. A user should never have to rely on memory for something the application can 'remember'.

JAD workshops

You and the users first need to gain experience with as many GUI products as possible. You need to learn from both good and bad products. What makes the good products intuitive? What makes the bad products difficult to use? Although some things can appear attractive at first sight, they can become tiresome with use (for example, too many different colors), so use various GUI products over a period of time.

Joint application design (JAD) workshops should involve users with GUI experience. In the first stages use a whiteboard to experiment with ideas for layout, window size and overall appearance. Then produce a mock-up using the development tool and from then on make changes directly in the development tool.

High-level design

First list all the objects based on the logical data model produced during the analysis stage, then list all the actions based on the task analysis and finally create an object–action matrix (for example, your objects might be 'Customer', 'Order Form' and 'Customer List', and your actions 'Create', 'Delete' and 'Print').

Next, list the windows and specify any drag and drop operations.

Specify the menu bars that will contain the actions. In general, try to allow any action at any time. This means you should avoid graying out menu bar items.

Finally specify the hierarchy of modal windows.

Low-level design

Describe a template object-list window and describe how common actions are invoked. An object-list window is one that displays a list of objects, such as a list of customers or orders.

For each object-list window, document the common actions that can be performed (for example, by menu or push-button) and any special actions and how they are invoked (for example, by double clicking on an object).

For each object window, list the attributes to be displayed and indicate which attributes can be updated. List the appropriate controls – buttons, entry fields, list boxes and so on. List the valid values, where appropriate, and finally list all the actions and how they are invoked.

Programming methods

The programming methods depend on the development tool being used. The following guidelines have been written assuming that the tool can produce dynamically loaded and linked modules. This requirement is essential for any client/server development tool that is going to be used by a team of developers.

Module architecture

The correct architecture for the application depends on the style of the user interface, the size of the application, and the desired balance between ease of maintenance and performance. There are three approaches:

- Type 1 (Module loading on start-up). The complete application is loaded at start-up. This will give good response times once all the modules are loaded, but the delivery platform must have enough memory to run all the applications. This architecture is best suited to small applications of up to about 50 modules. It is the easiest structure to build but not the easiest to test and debug.

- Type 2 (Module loading on use). The application consists of a small base module. This is a group of modules that provide a framework. The base modules will include global variables, data definitions and common utilities such as exception handling and help. Most of the modules are dynamically loaded and unloaded following certain user events such as selecting an item from a menu, a push-button or a double-click event. The application can be extended easily by adding modules. The modules are easy to debug and can be developed and tested independently.

- Type 3 (Object-based or Component programming). The system consists of many application components. Each component represents a business object, such as a customer list, an order form or a supplier. Each object is implemented as a small set of modules, as in type 1 above. An object can be started independently from the desktop or by another object. Objects communicate using a messaging interface. This object-oriented approach is the most flexible for system growth but the performance and messaging overhead depends on the tool and operating system used.

Structured programming

Each procedure should be kept short, strongly structured and easy to read and understand. Programming standards should be strictly enforced.

The aim is always to develop a procedure so that it can be understood and maintained by anyone coming along later. An important aspect of this is good commenting and good documentation.

When developing any large application (and all client/server applications tend to be large) it is essential either to maintain accurate, up-to-date documentation or to use an impact analysis tool. This is because as the system grows, you will need to understand the effect that changing one part of the system has on another.

Questions that good documentation or an impact analysis tool should be able to answer are:

- Where is this variable, data structure, procedure or function used throughout the system?

- How is it used? For example, is it displayed, updated or just referenced?

- Does every item displayed have the same style, format and validation?

- Are data structures and procedures commented?

- Where are the different classes of procedure defined (for example, double-click procedures, menu procedures and so on)?

- Are any variables or procedures unused?

Naming standards

Variables, data structures and procedures should have a consistent naming convention. The name of a procedure has three attributes: its type (display, menu, double-click, SQL . . .), the action (view, create another, save, undo . . .) and the object (customer, car, car lot, order form . . .). Sometimes it is useful also to include the name of any relevant window, especially if windows are separately named.

An action or object should always be spelled the same way in all procedures. Actions and objects should be given the same name as in the user interface, but a shortened version of the name may be used if it is spelled consistently.

Version control

A version control product, such as Intersolv's PVCS, should be used to control module development. Programmers 'check-out' modules they wish to work on and then 'check-in' the modules when finished. When one developer is using a module, no other developers can work on it at the same time.

The version control software can keep track of milestone points, and can backtrack to any previous point if a regression is found after a series of changes are made.

It is good practice to avoid splitting development into parallel lines (when you have two versions of one or more modules). Everyone should be working on a single set of source code towards the next agreed version.

Testing

It is recommended that a software test tool such as Mercury's WinRunner, Microsoft's MSTEST, Softbridge's ATF or SQA's Robot is used. Test scripts and test data need to be planned and started during the design stage.

There should be a separate test team responsible for producing and running the test plan. The test plan is a written document specifying a series of different types of tests that must be applied to each new version. It will include running scripts against standard data, performance measurement and manually trying to break the system (sometimes called 'black team testing').

Test data should be realistic and there should be realistic volumes, and performance testing on the final delivery platform should start at the earliest possible stage.

Distribution

The procedure for releasing updates to finished applications is more involved than for mainframe development because the application is distributed.

The application code would normally be stored on a file server and loaded across the LAN when required. This means that the central organization responsible for release control only needs to update the application on the server.

If such an organization is not in place, create one responsible for release control and end-user support.

Distribution to a small number of users on a LAN is straightforward and the issues around installing new versions are the usual ones – user training, backward compatibility and database conversion.

Distribution to remote branch networks will be based on electronic file down-load, possibly controlled by a software distribution product. This can be done either by physically sending disks for local installation or by down-loading the files. Important considerations in making the choice are the availability of skilled staff locally, the time and cost of the transfer, the compatibility between upgrades and the timing of new releases. If all sites must switch to a new version on a given day then the logistics of conversion become more complex. The conversion must be done overnight or over a weekend on all sites. This may involve installing the new version alongside the old well in advance and the system switching between them on a given date. The new versions need to aim for backward compatibility.

Because of the risks inherent in this type of switch, it is better to make changes that are compatible with old versions. In this way different sites can run with different levels of application software and the upgrade can be carried out incrementally.

If you are doing phased development it is a good idea to complete all the phases before rolling out to more than one remote LAN.

The other aspect of delivery to consider is the increased load on the support desk. The support desk plays a vital role in ensuring the success of the application. The support staff need to combine the skills of mainframe and PC support staff, that is, they must understand what can go wrong with an autonomous PC on a LAN and they must also understand the application issues. It is recommended that a help desk system for call logging and tracking be built.

The application should be supplied with a complete on-line help system including text, graphics and hypertext links. This should be seen as an extension of the support desk. It is recommended that the help system should explain the use of the total application, rather than just which key to press and when. This will reduce the level of support calls.

Some do's and don'ts

- DO start! This is the only way to learn. It is a mistake to spend too long working out standards and procedures or working on a paper specification.

- DO keep flexible. If you are starting your first project of this type, measure and analyse what you are doing and if it is not working, change it.

- DO involve the end-user from the start of the project and get feedback by building a pilot application first.

- DO take the database design off-line and make it the responsibility of someone with the skills of a database administrator.

- DO make use of the SQL data definition language. If you are not using a database design tool (and probably even if you are) the database design will not be correct first time. So put all your 'create' statements into a single program, together with the equivalent 'drop' statements. Then redesigning and reconstructing your database becomes fast and simple.

- DO use your best people to implement the application but ensure they write guidelines for the other people who will be developing client/server applications later.

- DO have the project team working closely with the Technical Group (a group of technology specialists with a good grasp of business issues and market directions). If necessary set up a Technical Group.

- DO plan all aspects of delivery of the finished application and new releases.

Here are the things to avoid:

- DO NOT launch into a major project using existing mainframe development standards. To reap the benefits of the graphical user interface, a more flexible and interactive approach is needed with the end-user.

- DO NOT get the user to sign off on a fixed specification at the start. The conventional 'waterfall' model of development demands a fixed, clearly defined specification that the user department signs off before design, programming and testing begin. Rapid development tools enable a prototype to be developed instead of such a specification. This prototype is likely to become the finished application.

- DO NOT leave the programmers to code from the specification. The people on the project should be business analysts who can program, or programmers with a good understanding of the business.

- DO NOT set up a complete team of junior programmers or committed systems programmers.

- DO NOT treat SQL as simply a high-level database access language. If you have not used SQL before, recruit someone with SQL experience before starting. The SQL language looks enticingly easy to learn, but it hides many pitfalls and dangers for the unwary. Issues like security, integrity, units of work and performance need to be planned from the start.

- DO NOT treat the graphical user interface as a way of displaying a sequence of (white) 3270 screens. The typical mistake is either to put too much or too little on a window. It is a good idea to copy examples of effective user interaction from other products you have seen, and get on to the team those people with experience in developing applications with GUIs.

The project that failed

To help consolidate the points made, the following is a 'case study' that shows how things can go badly wrong on a project.

A big company's IT department decided to down-size an existing 3270 application and give it a GUI. The staff had no experience with PC development, so they decided to bring in contract staff with C++ programming experience. The IT department took the advice of the contractors and decided to write the application in C++.

To save money, they sent only the company's staff to the relevant training courses. They then spent two months putting together the basics of the low-level libraries needed. A budget was approved to develop the whole system in six months.

The project was named GUSTO.

Six months later, they were just starting to write the SQL. The Database Administrator for their DB2 database had no time to help on the project. No one else on the project had any experience of writing SQL, but they picked up the basics by reading the supplier's documentation.

The first version was shown to the users, who had not been involved at all in the project. The users were extremely enthusiastic and inundated the project team with requests for changes.

After another six months, performance remained terrible and they asked an outside SQL consultant to help. The consultant recommended changes to the data model and the use of static SQL. The changes were difficult to make, but after a further two months they were finished and performance improved dramatically.

It was then estimated that if three months were to be spent writing a user interface class library, then all the users' new requests could be completed in just one further month. Three months later, the library had not been completed and it was estimated that the application would take two months to convert to the new libraries before the enhancements could be started. The finance director looked at total expenditures and canceled the project.

An unhappy story, but now let us look at what was happening down the road.

The project that succeeded

At the same time, a rival company had also started a client/server project. The IT department was asked to build a system to provide potential customers with 'while-you-wait' sales information and quotes. The basic business requirement was to improve customer service by reducing the time needed to produce a proposal from three weeks to three days.

A 4GL was selected and a contract programmer with SQL experience recruited. The whole team was sent on the development tool supplier's one-week training course. They asked the tools supplier to provide three weeks of consultancy to get them started in the right direction.

Two branch staff were added to the project and one month was spent on data modeling and building a demonstrator. To gain experience with good GUI design, they spent time using a number of GUI personal productivity tools.

The project was named SAILS.

A pilot system was started and three months later a simple system was available with which the head-office branch could view sales information. Fifty 486 PCs were ordered for the next phase.

A programmer's guidebook was produced and the complete system was estimated to take a further nine months. Weekly code 'walkthroughs' were organized and the test team started preparing test data and test plans.

Four months later, a version was released for producing proposals, although

Tel: +44 (0) 932 772266

Fax: +44 (0) 932 771499

I hope you found this book informative. If you are now planning to start a client/server project further information is available. Please send this reply paid card or fax for:

- ● A free demonstration disk ☐
- ● Information about AM, the Client/Server development tool ☐
- ● Additional case studies ☐

Name: ....

Title: ....

Company: ....

Address: ....

....

Tel. Number: .... Fax. Number: ....

---

intelligent ENVIRONMENTS

proven client/server solutions

Tel: (508) 640 1080

Fax: (508) 640 1090

I hope you found this book informative. If you are now planning to start a client/server project further information is available. Please send this reply paid card or fax for:

- ● A free demonstration disk ☐
- ● Information about AM, the Client/Server development tool ☐
- ● Additional case studies ☐

Name: ....

Title: ....

Company: ....

Address: ....

....

Tel. Number: .... Fax. Number: ....

Intelligent Environments
Freepost (SW 1387)
Crystal House, P.O. Box 51
Sunbury-on-Thames
Middlesex TW16 5BR
United Kingdom

BUSINESS REPLY MAIL
FIRST CLASS   PERMIT NO. 1   TEWKSBURY, MA

POSTAGE WILL BE PAID BY ADDRESSEE

NO POSTAGE
NECESSARY
IF MAILED
IN THE
UNITED STATES

Intelligent Environments
2 Highwood Drive
Tewksbury
MA 01876

data could not be saved. Four months after that, the system was in use in a pilot branch and the average turnaround for sending out proposals was measured at two days. Customer reaction was excellent and the level of business at that branch jumped more than 25%.

The finance director approved an increase in the project budget so that all branches would have the system installed by the end of the fiscal year.

Summary

Building client/server systems offers organizations the opportunity to introduce more responsive development methods that can help the users become more involved in the process.

The objective is to develop applications that make the organization more profitable by making the users more effective. The increased effectiveness comes from the use of a responsive GUI combined with direct access to corporate data. The design of the user interface is therefore key to achieving the business objective. This was not true when developing mainframe applications.

Creating an effective user interface means working closely with the user and trying alternatives. This leads to a new style of working called joint application development (JAD) or iterative development. For JAD to work changes requested by the user must be capable of being made very quickly and this requires the use of rapid application development (RAD) tools.

This chapter describes the type of methodology that should be used to control a project using JAD with RAD tools. Rapid development does not imply controls should be dropped. On the contrary, control of rapid change requires more discipline in the application of change control.

Also, the use of easy-to-learn tools does not mean that close attention does not need to be taken of the architecture, design, data integrity, security and performance considerations.

Guidelines, hints and tips are given but real knowledge comes from doing the job yourself. Therefore, the best advice is to get started as soon as possible.

CHAPTER 6

CASE STUDIES

All the following case studies are based on live applications that have been developed in the US and Europe using a 4GL called AM. Further details can be obtained by completing the reply-paid card in this book.

They show how a variety of organizations in different sectors and with different requirements achieved business benefits through the use of client/server technology.

Fireman's Fund Insurance

Business requirement	Technical requirement
High performance	Use combination of APPC with IMS and SQL
Up-load to existing mainframe application	Use 3270 emulation
Rapid development	High-level 4GL

Commercial Workstation manages flow of information for better business decisions

Fireman's Fund Insurance Company has turned to client/server computing to make better business decisions and service its customers faster. The Noveto, California insurer writes $3 billion in annual premiums across the US. The company's Commercial Division is deploying new capabilities that enable its underwriters and managers to process business more efficiently and better understand insurance risks.

Improving the decision-making process

Bad risks directly impact profitability. Insurers must be able to understand the nature of each risk and determine the appropriate premium for it. Such decisions need to be based on accurate and complete information, and to service customers better, they must be made quickly.

'In the past, Fireman's Fund underwriters relied on a manual system – and decisions were at times based on incomplete information,' said Chris McDermott, Director of Commercial Insurance Systems. Chris and his team of 12 were tasked with developing an application to improve underwriting decisions. Termed the Commercial Workstation, the new client/server application

> 'moves the right information to the right people faster,' said Chris.

In choosing a development environment, Fireman's Fund's criteria were straightforward: they did not want to be bound to C programming, and they needed rapid application-development capabilities. Selecting AM as the Commercial Workstation development tool

> 'really helped us get into client/server computing quickly,' said Chris.

Integrating team members

Fireman's Fund's underwriters work with raters, who calculate premiums, together with a processing staff, which prepares the printed policies and supporting documents.

Chris and his developers undertook the Commercial Workstation project to enable these teams of professionals to manage the way they process 'cases' more effectively. Cases are commercial customers that are applying for, changing, or renewing coverage.

Key to the power of the Commercial Workstation is its Inbox, which gives Commercial Division professionals a simple yet powerful way to manage their cases and associated data. Using the Inbox, an underwriter can open any case and look at all relevant policy and underwriting information. Among the types of information available might be financial reports, driving records, physical property descriptions, and corporate safety-program details. By examining such characteristics, underwriters can identify levels of risk and define appropriate premiums.

Simplifying data access

The application simplifies access to this information. Pull-down options on the Inbox action bar let users down-load information from IBM host databases to LAN-based RDS databases.

Access is fast as well. An IMS transaction is triggered on the host via APPC communications, and information is sent through SQL calls to populate the local RDS database. Although commercial policies can be very large – some approaching 100 000 bytes of data – file transmissions typically take less than 20 seconds.

When team-members have completed all actions on a case, the updated policy data is up-loaded to the host. This takes place via an EHLLAPI application also written in AM, which can run as a background task.

Managing workflow

The 4GL helped Chris's group develop Inbox capabilities in an iterative fashion, working closely with users to gather input and feedback. Flexible workflow-management capabilities are the result.

For instance, as a case moves from underwriter to rater and from rater to processing staff, it can be categorized by priority or required action. A 'rush' or 'suspend' status can be placed on a case. Filtering capabilities then allow team-members to select and sort their cases. Then as a case moves to each successive Inbox, instructions can be defined for the next person. Cases can also be reassigned by managers based on individual workloads.

Smart forms reduce errors

To further simplify processing and improve the quality of decisions, Chris's team developed a 'smart-forms' capability.

'We've electronically captured dumb forms',

said Chris about the various standard forms that are used in preparing policies. The forms are now provided on-line with each case.

Each form automatically includes any information that exists in the database – policy number, customer address and so on. Users can then make modifications and add text – for example, a note reminding the customer to forward information on a previous carrier. The forms are then used to generate letters to customers.

Nationwide deployment

Fireman's Fund has deployed the Commercial Workstation at six sites throughout the US. It currently processes 75% of Fireman's Fund's small-business commercial insurance.

The AM-developed application will eventually be deployed at 12 locations. Said Chris,

> 'when you can request a file from the host in 20 seconds, and pass it on to the next person in a fraction of a second – you can do a much better job of servicing the customer. Business is processed faster, with less staff – which reduces expense and lowers premiums for our customers'.

Grossman's

Business requirement	Technical requirement
Simplify store reordering	Direct SQL link to DB2 on mainframe
Simplify goods receipt in store	Direct hand-held radio transmission
Improve point-of-sale service	Registers with direct database access via satellite
Reduce credit sale time from 30 seconds to 4 seconds	Direct credit card scan, credit access and mainframe look-up
Low-risk development using existing mainframe programmers	Easy-to-learn 4GL

Grossman's rolls out chain-wide replenishment systems

The 120-unit, $800 million Grossman's home center chain has developed an enterprise-wide cooperative processing architecture. The environment is built around the retailer's DB2 mainframe relational database, satellite network with LAN support, PC point-of-sale (POS) systems, and wireless hand-helds. The architecture has allowed Grossman's to rapidly roll out new inventory tracking, replenishment and customer service applications.

This architecture was developed in support of a new corporate strategy, defined with the aid of McKinsey & Company, for improved customer service. The company embarked on a program to upgrade its replenishment capabilities to better accommodate the needs of professional contractors and serious 'do-it-yourself' customers in its northeastern US stores. This project required new systems and network improvements.

The following is a description of components of the new enterprise-wide system.

DB2-based replenishment system

The system resides on a Hitachi Data Systems EX-50 mainframe host. The system incorporates models designed specifically for Grossman's by statistician Harvey Wagner at the University of North Carolina. These models reflect studies of the behavior of Grossman's basic product categories.

Based on these models and established merchandise planograms of shelves in each store, the system automatically determines the quantity of merchandise to order. This recommendation involves four steps:

(1) Create forecast indexes. This step reviews up to three years of sales history to calculate a monthly volume index, a three-season volume index, a promotional volume index, and three-season safety stock based on planograms and actual sales.

(2) Update forecasts. Each week the system brings in the previous week's sales and forecasts the next 16 weeks. The forecast uses the indices and the previous 52 weeks of sales history.

(3) Plan replenishment. The replenishment system subtracts from each store's requirements the on-hand and on-order merchandise daily. It then rounds the orders off to pack size and minimums to determine order quantity.

(4) Place purchase orders. Finally, based on the order placement schedule, the replenishment system then sends orders to vendors and distribution centers via electronic data interchange. The system also produces reports on needs not met by vendors.

The new, multi-tasking POS systems include standard, off-the-shelf hardware components and in-house-written application software.

The POS is built around an NCR 3000 Series PC with Microchannel Bus, 16 megabyte RAM and 160 megabyte disk storage. In addition, the hardware incorporates a 7052 keyboard, a 14-inch NCR VGA monitor, an Epson thermal printer, a Checkmate micro check reader, a magnetic stripe reader, and a CCD scanner.

Grossman's developed its POS applications and screens with AM. This tool allows for object-oriented programming, prototyping and modular development on PCs across LANs. The tool creates applications with graphical user interfaces, and enables access via SQL calls.

Grossman's developed its basic POS applications in less than six months. The applications include sales transactions, special sales screens, price look-up, refunds, suspended sales and delivery scheduling. In addition, each system 'hot keys' for data retrieval from a DB2 database for customer account information and merchandise in-stock position.

Enterprise-wide network

Grossman's selected Hughes Network Systems, Inc. to provide a comprehensive, interactive satellite network linking its stores with its corporate database. The contract is valued at approximately $1.5 million.

Hughes installed a one-meter Personal Earth Station very small aperture terminal (VSAT) atop each retail outlet to link with Grossman's corporate data center in Randolph, Massachusetts. Two-way data traffic is routed from mainframe computer to Hughes' shared hub earth station, and then via satellite, to the stores.

According to Grossman's, the new PC–POS software will automatically debit a store's inventory when a product is purchased, triggering automatic reorder when the merchandise stock reaches a pre-determined level. The new approach greatly simplifies the store's ordering process, which was previously accomplished manually. The company's receiving operations will also benefit from direct satellite access via small, hand-held radio transmitters that will log in arriving merchandise by purchase order number as it is received.

Other point-of-sale applications handled over the satellite link include check and credit authorization, formerly accomplished via dial-up network in a process that typically took 30–45 seconds. Satellite transmission has already reduced this delay to about four seconds.

Using Hughes' LANAdvantage interface, the Token Ring network, comprising hundreds of PCs, gains transparent access to the remote mainframe over the dedicated satellite links. This will allow contractors to access information about their credit records or make payments on accounts in any store.

IBM

Business requirement	Technical requirement
Present miles of documentation clearly	OS/2 + hypertext + multimedia
Integrate to mainframe data	4GL with good communications and database facilities
Integrate multiple applications on the PC	Good inter-program communication facilities

Automobile and aircraft maintenance

The maintenance of any sophisticated equipment typically is supported by a whole library of technical documentation. Examples are:

- Service manuals

- Illustrated parts catalogues

- Wiring diagrams

- Troubleshooting manuals, and so on

For a typical airline's fleet of aircraft, the volume of paper is enormous. Piled page on page, it would reach well over 50 000 feet – over the flight ceiling of most aircraft, and weigh more than a Jumbo Jet.

Of course an airline fleet management's top three priorities are safety, safety and safety. However, there are other considerations – not the least of which are maintenance efficiency and economy.

That much of the technical documentation is still in paper form may seem surprising, but then it should be remembered that the service life of an airliner is well over 20 years. Until recently the most practical way to deliver this volume of documentation to its many geographically spread users was in paper form. Worse still, because it is impractical for the person on the shopfloor to carry whole books around, those parts that are needed for the task in hand must be photocopied, resulting in a further mountain of paper.

But this is all changing. New planes, like the Airbus 340, the Fokker 100, the Boeing 747 400, and the exciting new Boeing 777 are designed, developed and built from the ground up using the most sophisticated computer technologies. The companies building these aircraft, together with their hundreds of suppliers and their airline customers, all work together throughout a new aircraft's development. Not only is electronic technical document flow an essential ingredient of this cooperation, but computer-based aircraft servicing documentation is an important product.

Such documentation, created and used as it is by many disparate organizations, must conform to recognized standards. For the civil aviation industry, the relevant standard for aircraft maintenance manuals is Air Transport Association (ATA) 100. Not only does this specify the detail of how to perform each maintenance task, but what tools are required, what materials, what skills, what access panels have to opened, whether electrical power is required (and where from), and a whole host of other parameters.

Well, there is no shortage of data! But how can it best be presented to the user?

IBM's Technical Viewer/2

TV/2 is IBM's product designed specifically to deliver this sort of information to the user. Operating in the OS/2 environment, TV/2 allows a user to navigate productively around a library of information using hypertext and search facilities familiar to anyone who uses OS/2's Help facility (IPF).

Not only does TV/2 allow a user to browse through volumes of textual information; electronic documents can contain all sorts of media – pictures of course, line drawings, color images, photographs, but also sound, animated diagrams and full motion video using IBM's Multimedia product range.

So in addition to providing easy access to information without the paperwork, TV/2 can enhance 'normal' technical documents with color, sound, video and more. If a mechanic needs a refresher course on how to adjust the liftdumper overcenter sensors (and who doesn't), not only can that person read the relevant information on-line, but can also get an on-demand video training course.

Well this gives a super information delivery mechanism. But the *real* benefits can be achieved if such information can be integrated into an overall information technology framework. How can this be achieved?

AM

One of the real strengths of TV/2 is its ability to be integrated into an application program. Not only does TV/2 provide programmed access to a vast library of hypermedia information, but TV/2 can inform the application about what the user is doing.

For instance in an Illustrated Parts Catalogue application, the user may select an aircraft engine model type. TV/2 displays an illustration of the engine. The user clicks the section to be worked on. An enlarged 'exploded' view of the section is displayed, with all parts numbered. In a separate window, the parts are listed, showing part number, description, quantity and so on. By clicking on a part (either on the diagram or in the list), the application is informed of the user selection, passing details such as part number, supplier and so on.

The AM application can then use this information to send a transaction, say, to a host DB2 system to locate and order the required parts, and to display parts availability to the user.

IBM chose AM as its preferred development environment for TV/2 applications. AM is recognized as a leader in its support of OS/2 functionality (including database and communications support), and it can be recommended to IBM's customers with the confidence that it will stand up in critical industrial applications.

A typical aircraft maintenance planning application would use the power of AM to combine TV/2 functionality and ATA 100 data structures together with aircraft service history to help the maintenance planner to answer such questions as:

- What is the next scheduled service for this aircraft, when is it due and where should it be performed?

- What maintenance tasks must be performed?

- Are there any unscheduled tasks, repairs and so on?

- How should these best be scheduled:
  – to optimize use of skills?
  – to minimize time in hangar?
  – to make most effective use of specialized tools?

- What access panels have to be opened?

- While required access panels are open, what other checks and so on could or should be performed to reduce future downtime?

During this planning process the application is recording all the requirements – tools, people, materials, spare parts and so on – when and where they are required, and for how long. This information is then used to build a 'just in time' warehouse picking list, and provide input to the manpower schedule to ensure that when the aircraft comes in for maintenance, everything is in place to provide complete and efficient handling, and a rapid return to safe fare-paying service.

Footnote

This section was kindly supplied by IBM and more details of IBM's Technical Viewer/2 product, and how it can be used in the airline, automotive, utilities, power tools and other industries, can be obtained from IBM, by calling Alan Malsher:

Phone: +44 (0)703 629123

Fax: +44 (0)703 629465

emsil: GBIBM5QL at IBMMAIL

or vnet: MALSHER at WINVMD

Mercedes-Benz Car Financing

Business requirement	Technical requirement
Easy-to-use system	Graphical user interface
Rapid delivery	High-productivity 4GL
Quality and reliability	Operating system with memory protection
Reduce time for proposal approval	Dial-up access to AS/400
Long life	Operating system with a long life

Car financing for dealers

Mercedes-Benz launched a new financial service for their dealers at the UK Motor Show in October 1990. The system is called Finance Link and partially automates the selling process and provides a standard mechanism for applying for car finance from the car maker.

The Finance Link system was designed to fit in with the overall company philosophy of Mercedes-Benz. Although demand for cars and for finance is in something of a state of flux, Mercedes-Benz believed after researching the market that its reputation for quality and reliability would make its financial services as popular as its vehicles.

Mercedes-Benz took the decision in December 1989 to set up Finance Link. The way that customers sought finance for new vehicles in the past was fairly time-consuming, with a dealer taking a customer's details on paper, handing the forms to a visiting representative of a finance company who would then take them back to the head office and enter them into a host system. Then it would take even longer for the finance company to reach a decision.

As a new company offering finance direct to its customer, Mercedes-Benz Finance wanted to streamline the process by capturing sales details at the dealer's showroom.

> 'We wanted to provide vehicles and finance from a single source, instead of using a third-party company,' explained Gordon Greenwood, Manager, Information Systems. 'Other car manufacturers, such as Fiat, offer automated customer finance, but there is usually a high street financing company on the other end of the network, rather than the car company itself.'

Front-ending AS/400s

Initially, Mercedes-Benz brought in Andersen Consulting to set up its systems. There were no hard and fast examples to follow.

> 'In Italy, the dealer will take the customer down to the coffee shop to clinch the deal. In the UK, the deal is usually done on the dealer's premises', said Mark Lewis, management consultant with Andersen.

Finance Link was designed to fit in with that model. Each dealership is given software running on an IBM PS/2 Model 55. Where deals have to be made on the customer's premises, such as when a company buys a fleet of vans, the sales person can take Finance Link to the site on a laptop.

Andersen Consulting began the design in January 1990. It started out with a clean sheet of paper, although it had to connect new applications to the main administration systems held on Mercedes-Benz UK's IBM 3090 mainframe. Andersen began by designing the back-end processing systems for Mercedes-Benz Finance. After a false start with a Swedish financial system that proved not to be sufficiently anglicized, Mercedes-Benz installed a package from Andersen itself called Leasepac. Running on an AS/400, this system is designed to sit in between the dealers' PS/2s and the IBM 3090. Mercedes-Benz Finance did not consider a network-based system for corporate applications.

> 'We still need the power of a minicomputer for the finance system', explained Lewis.

Twenty-fold productivity gains

The front-end to Finance Link had to be as easy as possible to use, with pull-down menus and color-coded controls. Mercedes-Benz wanted to give the dealers the reassurance that they needed to begin using the system.

The PC part of the system also had to have powerful multi-tasking and communications facilities.

A third factor in the equation was that Mercedes-Benz Finance wanted to go live by the end of 1990, so it needed a tried-and-tested system as quickly as possible.

Lewis knew about AM because he had seen it being used on other Andersen projects. He knew that using the software could speed up the development process as much as twenty-fold over native Presentation Manager code.

> 'We wanted to put in OS/2 rather than MS DOS application programs because we wanted a system that would carry Mercedes-Benz Finance through the 1990s and beyond', said Lewis.

As a leading development tool, AM was the natural partner to IBM's Extended Edition version of OS/2.

Putting the customer first

Finance Link includes three main screens. The first shows details of the car and can display complete lists of optional models and extras such as a fridge in the trunk of the car. The second displays details of finance deals available, such as lease or buy, repayments, residual value after a lease is completed and the length of time it takes to pay for a vehicle. The third screen accepts details of the prospective customer. It was a deliberate policy to follow this path, rather than asking for the customer's details first.

> 'A lot of customers come in for a quote', said Lewis. 'You could put them off by asking for private details first'.

Mercedes-Benz relied on its Finance Link system to help it reach its first year business volume target of 120 million pounds. By using IT to make the provision of finance easier, it hopes to be able to gain significant commercial benefits. Dealers will be able to give the customers a decision on financing quickly, thereby swaying customers from seeking financing elsewhere. It was crucial that Mercedes-Benz was able to develop its Finance Link system quickly with AM.

In the coming decade, the companies that succeed will need to be able to respond to customer demand as fast as possible. Japanese car manufacturers have shown that it is possible to build flexible, more responsive organizations that can react quickly to changes in the market. Companies which trade in information will need to follow the same kind of model.

Minnesota Mutual

Business requirement	Technical requirement
Reduce lead fulfillment from 3 weeks to 3 days	On-line client/server to mainframe DB2
Develop application rapidly	High productivity 4GL
Handle complex data input	GUI for list selections and validations
Maintain mainframe performance and security	Use static SQL and DDCS/2
Develop using teams	4GL with good team support and modular development
Test using local database, not mainframe	Test using DB2/2, switch to DB2 using DDCS/2
Offer new tailored services to customers	Flexible 4GL with rapid development and reusable code libraries

Building links to your customer

Widespread interest in down-sizing and re-engineering information systems is catalysing rapid growth in client/server computing. In fact, 75% of information executives in organizations with revenues in excess of $250 million are implementing or seriously considering this approach, according to a recent *Datamation* magazine survey.

Client/server makes business sense: it maximizes the use of powerful but low-cost graphical PCs and is ideally suited for networks that include existing mainframes and mid-range systems. Many companies are looking for ways to leverage its power, especially for customer service.

For mission-critical customer service operations, client/server applications must access and integrate data from large, remote corporate databases. Today, corporate programmers are under pressure to develop these kinds of applications faster and with fewer resources. The traditional CASE (Computer Aided Software Engineering) tools used to build yesterday's mainframe-based projects now inadequately address application development in a client/server environment.

Despite these challenges, insurers are succeeding in applying client/server computing to build more effective customer service capabilities. Here is an account of how St. Paul-based Minnesota Mutual has implemented this technology.

Opportunities

With more than $106 billion of insurance in force, Minnesota Mutual Life Insurance Company ranks among the top 1% of insurance companies in the US and is a leading provider for mortgage-related insurance products through financial institutions.

Nearly three years ago, the company's Financial Services division, which services large banks and financial institutions, created a system to enhance the sale of home-owner's insurance to new mortgage loan applicants. As Frank FitzPatrick, Vice President of Customer Development, put it,

> 'Our goal was to provide a paperless, front-end marketing and administrative system that would allow us to market our products more rapidly, more efficiently and more effectively'.

Dubbed LINK (Lender Insurance Network), the system enables financial institutions to supply leads electronically to Minnesota Mutual, which then offers property/casualty insurance to interested consumers through telemarketing. In the 18 months since its introduction, nearly 200 financial institutions have taken advantage of the LINK service for home-owner's insurance.

The initial system was a resounding success. As a result, additional efforts were made to explore how LINK could further enhance revenue opportunities for Minnesota Mutual and its financial institution partners. It was decided to expand it to accommodate a second marketing channel – direct mail – as well as life and disability products.

Leading questions

The new system design called for LINK to receive all leads electronically from financial institutions, analyse them for completeness, and – depending on the marketing program established for each institution – pass the leads to a telemarketing group for follow-up telephone contact or to a direct mail group for package production and mailing.

The information that the new system would have to manage included insurance regulations impacting direct mail and telemarketing in each state, the array of Minnesota Mutual products each bank or financial institution wished to offer, and a wide range of fulfillment packages to be offered to consumers.

The Information Services (IS) staff knew that providing these additional capabilities would present a development challenge. For security, it was decided that all data should continue to reside on the IBM 3090 mainframe in the home office; therefore, any new development technology had to provide direct access to the company's mainframe-based, DB2 databases. Of equal importance was the ability to develop applications quickly. Another consideration was the nature of the data: selections for 50 states and thousands of customers.

First, the IS team considered a mainframe-based solution, but IS project manager Craig Andrew noted that the expanded LINK application

   'would have been nearly impossible to write on a mainframe'.

The complexity and volume of data dictated the need for a graphical user interface with list boxes and other devices for entering, validating and updating data quickly.

Next, the team explored the use of DOS-based PCs running as clients to the mainframe server. The available development tools, however, offered inadequate DB2 connectivity in a DOS environment.

Finding answers

Ultimately, the IS team decided to use AM because it enabled them to:

- Support different communications protocols and database options, ensuring that the applications they built for banks and financial institutions would integrate smoothly with Minnesota Mutual's mainframe environment.
- Exploit the power of high-powered, graphical, multi-tasking workstations.
- Develop applications in a visual programming environment, eliminating the need to learn a new language.

The team has implemented two AM-developed database applications: one manages the marketing plan information for each financial institution, including the Minnesota Mutual products to be offered and the promotion method chosen; the other the information about Minnesota Mutual's product lines, including information to assure compliance for all of their marketing efforts.

The lead processing component of the LINK system has no user intervention. Data entry staff use IBM PS/2 workstations – outfitted with 12 megabytes of memory – to maintain non-lead database information that includes additions, deletions and changes to insurance product information, regulations and laws. A local area network (LAN) connects the PS/2s, LAN database servers housing the data, and the IBM 3090 in the home office; the LAN software products are IBM's LAN Requester and Novell's NetWare.

As data is entered and updated, it is stored in IBM Database Manager tables on the OS/2 server. These tables are then used to populate DB2 database tables on the mainframe, using SQL statements passed via IBM's DDCS/2 software. All of the SQL statements are static, rather than dynamic; because static SQL is pre-compiled, it is fast and provides a high level of data security.

At night, each bank or financial institution transmits lead information (in flat files) to the LINK mainframe server, using standard communications software. Working against the DB2 tables populated by the AM applications, the LINK system determines which promotion method is appropriate – based on each client's marketing profile – and provides lead and product information to Minnesota Mutual's telemarketing or direct mail system.

Fulfillment packages are sent to all leads – either immediately on the direct mail system or after telephone contact by a telemarketing representative. The AM application electronically down-loads fulfillment package instructions for each lead to Minnesota Mutual's mailing vendor nightly. A package is in the mail within three days of receiving the lead.

A winning proposition

Everyone – Minnesota Mutual, its IS team, the banks and financial institutions, and policy owners – benefits from the new system. LINK has enabled them to:

(1) Streamline development. Although the IS team estimated that it would take two programmers 24 weeks to complete the new applications, they finished the job in 19 weeks. Of particular help was an AM feature called Dynamically Linked Modules, which enabled the two applications to use shared code for the functions they have in common.

Taking a client/server approach also simplified the testing process. Because of the compatibility between Database Manager and DB2, it was possible to conduct all testing locally, ensuring that the new applications would work with DB2 before being put into production.

As Minnesota Mutual adds additional products to the system in the future, it expects to leverage even greater productivity gains from the decision to build LINK on a client/server foundation.

(2) Deliver fast, flexible service – and performance – to their banking and financial customers. Minnesota Mutual's field force, marketing staff and IS team work closely with each financial institution to tailor the new system to its specific needs. In addition, LINK's flexibility allows these customers to pilot test mailings and to experiment with different products and promotion methods. The increasing variety of insurance products available via LINK also offers new opportunities for revenue. Finally, the on-line system has reduced the lead fulfillment process from three weeks to three days, improving considerably the level of service that can now be offered to these customers.

(3) Reach and satisfy new markets. Minnesota Mutual has plans for aggressive growth in the large financial institution marketplace throughout the US. This will enable it to meet the property/casualty insurance needs of new home-owners and to make them aware of a wide variety of products that are available to fund other major events in their lives. At the same time, LINK enables Minnesota Mutual to increase its roster of prospective clients and to cross-sell their entire line of products.

FitzPatrick sums up the system's flexibility, noting that LINK

'gives us the opportunity to customize a program for each institution, and to take advantage of the marketing opportunities that an electronic, paperless process affords'.

Used properly then, client/server can be the tie that binds customers to your organization. Minnesota Mutual has done just that, and everyone is reaping the rewards.

Schindler

Business requirement	Technical requirement
Access to 3090 mainframe data	4GL with good mainframe access
User productivity	Real multi-tasking
Low maintenance costs	Avoid OO programming
Avoid 3090 mainframe upgrade	Off-load work to PCs

Mastering change in declining markets

Schindler, the largest elevator and escalator manufacturing company in Europe, with an operating income of nearly $3 billion (over 4 billion Swiss francs) and more than 32 000 staff worldwide.

Being heavily dependent on real estate, the worldwide reduction in the start of new building work has cut the opportunity to install new elevators. The senior management of Schindler saw that the supply of accommodation, especially offices, was going to exceed demand for some time and therefore the company would need to concentrate on quality and the refurbishment sector of their market.

In a decreasing, more price-sensitive and diversifying market, Schindler needed to be even more adaptable and quality conscious. A number of steps were taken to ensure that Schindler maintained its number one position in Europe and aggressively competed in other markets.

Schindler's attention to detail and forward thinking have lead them to be awarded the maintenance contract for the 89 elevators and 20 escalators for the world's largest building, the Sears Tower in Chicago. Schindler's wholly owned subsidiary Millar was given the task of modernizing 60 elevators in the Empire State building.

In Spain, Schindler equipped the entire infrastructure of EXPO'92 in Seville with 213 elevators and escalators.

Adrian Bunter, the Manager of Application Development for Schindler Informatik, has the task of finding ways to improve the quality of information available within the group and of introducing better methods of keeping Schindler ahead of the competition.

One of his current projects in 1991 was to give the users, both in the headquarters at Ebikon (near Luzern in Switzerland) and those in the decentralized offices, better access to the information held on the company's mainframe.

Another was to reduce the downtime of elevators and escalators through improved and automated feedback of maintenance information from customers' sites – allowing Schindler's maintenance center to know of problems, and dispatch technicians, before they become critical.

Improved use of Schindler products

Since elevators and escalators need periodic maintenance, Schindler has expanded its remote emergency call and monitoring system (SERVITEL) by the integration of its computer aided maintenance system (CAMA) to improve the quality of service to their users. This allows more efficient planning of preventative maintenance and reduces the unplanned time when Schindler products are taken out of service, thereby increasing the quality of service provided.

Faster access to information

With the expansion of the use of the SAP accounts and logistics software on the IBM 3090, there was the requirement for users to have access to the large amount of information stored on the mainframe.

The SEE Project (Offer System for Export; estimated development effort 400 man-days) allows the quoting of costs for new elevators. The information required is stored in SAP but 50 different types of layout for presentation needed to be developed to allow the users to update and use the format they wanted.

One way to give access to the database on the 3090 was to increase the use of terminals for the decentralized offices throughout Switzerland. The other was to use intelligent workstations on a LAN.

> 'Schindler Aufzuge AG, Switzerland, one of the various group companies, maintains a customer database (of about 80 000 customers) centrally on the mainframe using SAP. The 13 decentralized offices also need to access the General Ledger information, preferably without using valuable CPU time on the mainframe', Adrian Bunter explained.

The need was for Bunter to find a cooperative processing and client/server solution which would fit in with the Schindler innovative approach to business, and also with existing investment in technology.

Choosing an operating system

The company was already using DOS on PCs and the choice for the new system was between Microsoft Windows or IBM's OS/2, and then how best to develop under the chosen system.

Bunter needed

> 'applications to be integrated with other applications on different platforms – the days of the standalone PC were numbered'.

So how did he choose between the omnipresent Windows and the lower profile OS/2.

> 'Windows' lack of interoperability with other platforms worried us. We needed a real multi-tasking operating system and OS/2 was much better in communication with heterogeneous platforms, which is very important from a developer's point of view', Bunter pointed out. 'It would have cost us a lot more to have tried to create a client/server solution with DOS or Windows since we would have needed to buy a lot of extra utilities. Therefore it would have been more expensive not to use OS/2'.

Which development tool?

Schindler has chosen the best products, in its opinion, for each task; and the Lotus products and SAP have all decided to go the CUA '91 route, so it was important that the users had the same functionality in their OS/2 development tool.

> 'We looked at all the other well supported development tools and ruled out all except for AM', said Bunter.

> 'Smalltalk didn't have a database interface at that time and we didn't want to go the Object Oriented route since that would give us long term maintenance problems with the Object Libraries. The Object Oriented concept is perfect for heavy graphics use but due to a lack of Object Oriented DBMS not for normal commercial use today'.

> 'Enfin was ruled out because of its Object libraries; you have different libraries for different applications, so we could see maintenance problems one or two years down the line. Also local support for the product was limited and there didn't seem to be many customers'.

> 'Easel was easy to rule out firstly on price, it was twice as much as anything else! Secondly , we would have had to take time to learn about PM events and we didn't want to have to become experts in PM and learn about the PM programming interface for OS/2'.

'Case PM was the only other real contender, but we didn't want C or COBOL and we wanted a total development tool with debuggers, tracers etc. We didn't want to develop all the communications ourselves'.

'Basically we didn't want to continue with a 3GL approach of generating code such as C or COBOL, we wanted a higher level approach'.

Finally Adrian Bunter was able to present his finding to the senior management of Schindler: AM was the best tool for the job.

Adrian Bunter's comments on the benefits of AM speak for themselves:

'The IBM 3090 is operational between the hours of 6 am and 6 pm for on-line database access – now with OS/2 we have 24 hour access, well almost', claimed Bunter. 'Reducing the load on the 3090 will save us money, it's not that we can down-size, but we don't have to upgrade it as soon as expected'.

'Another benefit is that using AM instead of COBOL has meant that we could increase the scope of the project. We have also experienced a time saving, which means we use the same budget but got a much better product as a result'.

'I hope to get all my developers using AM soon', said Bunter. 'When my budget allows. Overall our users get a much better service since we introduced AM on OS/2'.

A quote from Alfred N. Schindler about his business seems appropriate to Adrian Bunter's job:

'Except for God only the user sees us all the time'.

INDEX

About
Intelligent Environments

Intelligent Environments is a fast-growing international group of companies headquartered in the UK, with its International Head Office in London and offices in the USA, Germany and Scandinavia. Intelligent Environments develops and markets client/server application development software for commercial, business use.

AM, Intelligent Environments' client/server development tool, was launched in April 1989 and is now the world's foremost OS/2 tool, with an installed base across Europe and the USA in a multitude of Fortune 500 and Times 1000 companies.

In the USA, Intelligent Environments is headquartered in Boston and has offices in Los Angeles, Houston and Chicago. Over the past three years Intelligent Environments has built up a blue-chip user base in America and Canada and always features as a short-listed supplier in the vast majority of major OS/2 projects.

In Europe, a strong sales and support organisation has been developed from the company's UK headquarters in Sunbury, backed up by a large number of distributors, consultancies and software houses throughout Europe. AM is represented in all the major European markets and is the clear market-leader in the UK and Scandinavia.

The company has a wholly owned subsidiary in Germany, headquartered in Frankfurt. Intelligent Environments GmbH has enjoyed rapid growth as it capitalizes on the single biggest European software market.